kraft-tex Creations

Lindsay Conner

Sew 18 Projects *with* Vegan Leather

Print, Stitch, Paint & Design

stashBOOKS®

an imprint of C&T Publishing

Text, photography, and artwork copyright © 2019 by C&T Publishing, Inc.

Publisher: Amy Barrett-Daffin

Creative Director: Gailen Runge

Acquisitions Editor: Roxane Cerda

Managing Editor: Liz Aneloski

Editorial Compiler: Lindsay Conner

Editor: Katie Van Amburg

Technical Editor: Debbie Rodgers

Cover/Book Designer: April Mostek

Production Coordinator: Zinnia Heinzmann

Production Editor: Alice Mace Nakanishi

Illustrator: Aliza Shalit

Photo Assistants: Rachel Holmes and Greg Ligman

Photography by Kelly Burgoyne of C&T Publishing, Inc., unless otherwise noted

Published by Stash Books, an imprint of C&T Publishing, Inc., P.O. Box 1456, Lafayette, CA 94549

Library of Congress Cataloging-in-Publication Data

Names: Conner, Lindsay, 1983- author.

Title: Kraft-tex creations : sew 18 projects with vegan leather - print, stitch, paint & design / compiled by Lindsay Conner.

Description: Lafayette, CA : C&T Publishing, Inc., [2019]

Identifiers: LCCN 2019020913 | ISBN 9781617458569 (softcover)

Subjects: LCSH: Textile crafts. | Sewing. | Leather, Artificial. | Kraft paper.

Classification: LCC TT699 .C654 2019 | DDC 746.4--dc23

LC record available at https://lccn.loc.gov/2019020913

Printed in China

10 9 8 7 6 5 4 3 2 1

Acknowledgments

Thanks to the entire team at C&T Publishing—Liz, Katie, Debbie, Alice, Zinnia, April, Kelly, and Aliza—for inspiring us to be creative with beautiful books.

Thank you to all the contributors—this book would not be possible without your lovely projects! Thank you to Baby Lock sewing machines and C&T Publishing for supporting my creative work with products and notions. —*Lindsay*

About the Compiler

Lindsay Conner is a writer, editor, and modern quilter. Her books include *On the Go Bags—15 Handmade Purses, Totes & Organizers*; *Modern Bee—13 Quilts to Make with Friends*; and *The T-Shirt Quilt Book*; and her designs have appeared in many magazines. When she's not sewing, Lindsay keeps busy as an ambassador for Baby Lock sewing machines, and as a pattern designer. She lives in Indianapolis, Indiana, with her husband, son, and two lovable cats. Visit Lindsay online at lindsaysews.com and craftbuds.com.

Photo by Lindsay Hinderer

Contents

Quick Ideas 12

Projects 34

Normajean Brevik
Modern Art Necklace

Lindsay Conner
Journal Necklace

Sara Curtis
Magnetic Fridge Organizer

Mary E. Flynn
Rainbow Crossbody Bag

36

40

44

48

Mary E. Flynn
Accordion Card File Wallet

Linda Seeman-Korte
Funky Zipper Pouches

Susan Leath
Mini Suitcase

Susan Leath
Snappy Slim Wallet

62

68

74

80

Susan Leath
Tuck Flap Wallet

Lightning McStitch
Cut Mesh Bag

Colette Moscrop
Print and Stitch Purse

Vera Therrell
Baby Shoes

84

88

96

102

Introduction

The first time I touched kraft-tex, I wasn't sure what to make with it. These days, I'm not sure if there's anything you *can't* make from kraft-tex! I've made zipper pouches, gift tags, bag accents, an advent calendar, jewelry, and more. Every time I get on Instagram, I love to scroll through the projects tagged with **#krafttex** to see what unique creations people are making with this versatile material. I love seeing the personalized projects with text and images printed right on the material. Painting, embroidery, and other special treatments bring these kraft-tex creations to life!

Inside the pages of this book, you'll find projects from twelve designers that are specially designed to use with kraft-tex, the remarkable paper material that sews just like fabric! For simple projects, check out Quick Ideas (page 12) for some home decor items and accessories you can make in a pinch! If you're ready for more of a challenge, turn to Projects (page 34) and sew up stunning bags, wallets, jewelry, organizers, and more. You'll learn special tips and techniques for working with kraft-tex along the way. And all the projects in this book come with patterns (pages 106–112 or pullout pages P1 and P2) so you can easily make your own templates and get started.

We can't wait to see what you make with kraft-tex!

Lindsay Conner

All About kraft-tex

It's the rugged paper that looks, feels, and wears like leather—but sews, cuts, and washes like fabric! Meet kraft-tex, the paper-fabric hybrid that is strong enough to use for projects that get tough wear like bags, zipper pouches, and wallets. Construct the main body of your project with it, or use it as a textural accent for straps, bag bottoms, tags and labels, fringe, and more. This fiber-based material (also known as "vegan leather") gets a supple, crinkled texture when washed, but it doesn't lose its durability.

If you've never tried kraft-tex, you're in for a treat! Crafters, sewists, mixed-media artists, home decorators, and bookbinders will enjoy experimenting with this multiuse material. There are so many ways to design with kraft-tex, because it's the ideal surface to stamp, paint, draw, or inkjet print on. You can sew and embroider on it (by machine or by hand), fold it, weave with it, die-cut it, apply shiny wax onto it … the options are endless.

kraft-tex is available in sheets, rolls, and bolts and comes in a variety of colors.

Types of kraft-tex

BASICS: Original Unwashed
This unwashed kraft-tex has a smooth surface and is a bit stiff. It's available in five colors: Natural, Black, White, Stone, and Chocolate.

Swatches of kraft-tex Basics

Swatches of kraft-tex Vintage

VINTAGE: Prewashed & Ready to Sew
This prewashed kraft-tex has a textured surface and more flexibility than the Basics line. It's available in the five original colors: Natural, Black, White, Stone, and Chocolate.

DESIGNER: Hand-Dyed & Prewashed
This kraft-tex is softer and has a more leathery, textured appearance. It's now available in thirteen colors: Blue Iris, Crimson, Denim, Emerald, Greenery, Linen, Marsala, Moss, Orchid, Saffron, Sapphire, Tangerine, and Turquoise.

Swatches of kraft-tex Designer

BUYING KRAFT-TEX

You can buy kraft-tex in stores and online at C&T Publishing (ctpub.com/kraft-tex). kraft-tex can be purchased as individual colors by the roll and by the bolt or in sampler packs.

✓ **Rolls** in the Basics line measure 19″ × 1.5 yards (54″); rolls in the Vintage and Designer lines are smaller, measuring 18½″ × 28½″.

✓ **Bolts,** available in the Basics line only, measure 10 yards × 19″.

✓ **Sampler packs** are 8½″ × 11″ sheets in colors from one of the kraft-tex lines:

Basics Sampler: 10 sheets of 5 Basics colors

Vintage Sampler: 10 sheets of 5 Vintage colors

Designer Sampler: 6 sheets of 6 Designer colors (Blue Iris, Greenery, Marsala, Orchid, Tangerine, and Turquoise)

Essentials Sampler: 7 sheets of 7 Designer colors (Crimson, Denim, Emerald, Linen, Moss, Saffron, and Sapphire)

kraft-tex Sewing Tips

Helpful Tools

The following tools are used in many projects in this book, so be sure to have them on hand.

Sewing machine

Rotary cutter and self-healing cutting mat

Craft knife (such as an X-ACTO)

Scissors

Iron and ironing board

Alex Anderson's 4-in-1 Essential Sewing Tool* (by C&T Publishing) *or* the following individual tools: a finger-pressing tool (such as a bone folder), a turning tool, and a stiletto or awl

Fabric clips (such as Clover Wonder Clips) or binder clips

Sewing pins and safety pins (to use on fabric)

Hand-sewing needles

Pencil

Ruler

Acrylic quilting ruler

* The 4 tools in this one tool are a seam ripper, a stiletto, a presser, and a turner.

Washing, Drying, and Ironing

For some ideas and projects in this book, we recommend using kraft-tex that has been pre-washed. This helps soften it and makes it much easier to manipulate and turn inside out. For projects that are sewn flat and where the fabric is not turned, such as the Kyoto Clutch (page 18) or Celestial Coasters (page 30), the original, unwashed kraft-tex Basics works great!

For projects that recommend prewashing:

- **If you're using kraft-tex Designer or Vintage:** This comes prewashed and is ready to sew immediately. If you're using the kraft-tex straight from the roll and find it's curling up, iron it flat so that your pattern pieces are cut accurately.

- **If you're using kraft-tex Basics:** This is *not* prewashed, so it's recommended that you wash it at least once before starting a project that requires prewashing. (Also be sure to prewash fabric and trim if you plan on washing your finished project.)

WASHING

For best results, cut the large roll into smaller pieces before washing. Depending on your pattern, cut a piece of kraft-tex a couple of inches larger than the total amount of material you'll need. (You'll cut the individual pieces after washing.)

To wash the kraft-tex, first take your piece and scrunch it up well. The more you work it, the better your texture will be! Then, toss it in your washing machine and wash with warm or cold water, with or without detergent.

Note

kraft-tex Basic and Vintage colors don't run—you can wash them all together with no problem. However, the kraft-tex Designer is hand-dyed, so it should only be washed in cold water with like colors.

DRYING

After washing, scrunch up the wet kraft-tex again and put it in the dryer. Take it out of the dryer while still damp and then lay it flat to finish drying.

IRONING

Ironing the washed kraft-tex on the cotton setting before you measure and cut it will flatten it out for more accurate results. Don't worry, you won't lose that great distressed texture!

Cutting, "Pinning," and Sewing

You can cut kraft-tex with anything that cuts fabric or paper—you don't have to have any specialized tools. For many of the ideas and projects in this book, it is easiest to cut the kraft-tex with a rotary cutter and cutting mat. You'll also want to have a sharp pair of scissors on hand for cutting some of the smaller shapes, clipping corners, and trimming seam allowances.

Important: Be sure *not* to use pins, as they will leave visible holes in your finished project. Instead of pins, you can use fabric clips (such as Clover Wonder Clips), binder clips, basting glue, staples, or glue dots. (If you're using glue or staples, be sure to keep them within the seam allowance.) You might also try tacking pieces together with Fabri-Tac glue, because it instantly holds the pieces together. Just be very careful not to let the glue press out onto the visible sections—it is permanent.

kraft-tex is a paper product, and as with all paper products, it tends to dull blades and needles over time. If you can, designate a pair of scissors or a rotary cutter to use only on paper products and another to use strictly for fabric. Designate a sewing machine needle for use with kraft-tex and store the needle pinned to a scrap of kraft-tex when not in use.

Because kraft-tex perforates (similar to vinyl), it is best not to sew back and forth in one place too many times, or the material will tear. To secure the stitching at the beginning of a seam, place the presser foot and needle about ¼″ in along the seamline and stitch *backward* to the edge, and then proceed to sew forward along the seamline.

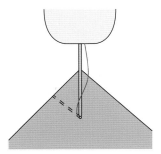

Always trim the corners and notch the curves before turning right side out to reduce bulk.

Press, press, press! Pressing your work sets the thread in the seams, creates a nice flat surface for the next step in your project, and the heat from the iron softens the kraft-tex and makes it easier to manipulate.

Note: The Right Side

kraft-tex doesn't have a true right or wrong side, but if you notice a texture difference between the sides, you may want to designate a "right" side to use consistently throughout your project.

Transforming kraft-tex with Surface Design

One of the amazing properties of kraft-tex is that it has endless possibilities for surface design: You can paint, stamp, dye, sketch, hand and machine stitch, glue, punch, appliqué, and print (with a computer printer) on it. The projects in this book show you some tried-and-true methods.

To print on kraft-tex with an inkjet printer, simply cut a sheet to size and send it through the printer tray. Use a test sheet of card stock or paper to check the placement of your design, then remove all other sheets of paper from the tray and print on the kraft-tex.

We're always learning new ways to create with kraft-tex, and as you experiment with it, you are likely to come up with various surface treatments that aren't covered in this book. A good resource is the Facebook group "Kraft Tex Junkies," where members ask and answer questions and share their own projects.

We hope the projects in this book inspire you to try something new, experiment with surface design, and have fun with all that kraft-tex has to offer!

Quick Ideas

Want to make something quick with kraft-tex?
These six ideas are fast to sew and are perfect to help you get
comfortable with the material before starting one of the more
challenging projects later in the book. Make little gifts, home decor, and
accessories from kraft-tex, and whet your appetite for more!

A

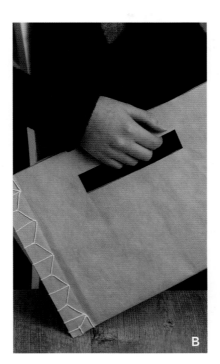

B

C

D

E

F

Seaside Luminary

Finished size: 3˝ wide × 3¼˝ tall × 3˝ deep

Inspired by a cozy, seaside town, these simple, watercolor-painted kraft-tex panels are decorated with cutout stars, allowing the light from the candle within to shine through. kraft-tex is a great watercolor painting surface, and it is sturdy enough to hold its form and be lashed with jute twine to complete the structure.

Photo by Odd Anders Brevik

About the Maker

Artist: Normajean Brevik

Blog: seasew.blogspot.com

Normajean is a fiber and mixed-media artist. Besides creating art, her favorite thing to do is teach and share her techniques and projects through her published works or her classes and lectures. She and her husband, Odd, travel extensively overseas as well as in the USA and Canada, which they enjoy exploring in their RV with their dachshund, Schotzie. Normajean seeks inspiration on their trips, often creating along the way. She looks forward to getting involved in the art community in her family's new home in Ormond Beach, Florida.

Materials

kraft-tex Basics or Vintage—White: 3¼″ × 12″

Votive candle and candle cup: 2½″ × 2½″ cup size (or use a small battery-operated tealight)

Watercolor paints and brush

Paper punch:

- *Star-shaped:* (Or use a craft knife to cut stars by hand.)
- *Round-hole:* ⅛″ size

Jute twine: 1 yard

Seashells: For corners

Hot glue gun

Clear-drying craft glue

Cutting

kraft-tex: Cut 4 rectangles 3″ × 3¼″ to paint individually, *or* paint the large rectangle (see Painting the Panels, below), then subcut into 4 panels 3¼″ × 3¼″. (For the second option, be sure to lightly mark where your panels will be cut.)

Make It

Painting the Panels

1. Using a pencil, mark a light line in the middle of the panels or strip for the *horizon line*. Divide the lower half by marking a second light line halfway between the horizon and the bottom on the panels or strip for the *water/sand line*.

2. Watercolor paint the scene, using the drag-and-skip method (see Note: Drag and Skip, page 16) and referring to the steps in the sections Sky, Sea, and Sand (pages 16 and 17) for individual painting instructions.

Note: Drag and Skip

Because this scene is mostly linear, I use what I call a drag-and-skip method of painting. This means leaving unpainted bits of canvas that allow the viewer to visualize clouds, waves, depth, and reflections of light. All areas of this scene will be painted in this technique.

Load the brush with the suggested color, beginning with the palest wash first (watercolors are painted from light to dark). Touch the loaded brush to the canvas and drag the paint for a short distance, lifting the brush in areas to leave unpainted parts. Paint the entire area, being sure to leave sufficient "skip" areas.

SKY

1. Begin with a very pale wash of blue from the top of the panel. Notice how your eye fills in "clouds" in the unpainted "skip" sections! Let dry.

2. Add a slightly darker wash of blue over parts of the light blue, being careful to leave some of the previous wash showing and also making sure the clouds stay unpainted/white.

3. For the third wash, use a very pale red (which reads pink) to suggest a sunset sky. Drag a few streaks of pink as a highlight. Paint the sky to the horizon line.

SEA

1. Begin at the horizon line with a pale/medium blue wash to paint the sea area. Continue to "skip" some areas to represent sun reflection and white wave crests. Paint until you reach the sand area, then drag a little rivulet of receding waves down into the sand area. Let dry.

2. Go back in with a darker wash of blue and, like the sky, add highlights, being sure not to paint out the white sun reflection and wave crests.

3. *Optional:* Add a few highlights of pale green-blue wash to give the sea more depth.

SAND

1. Paint with a pale wash of raw sienna color, using the drag-and-skip method to denote sun reflection and shadow from uneven sand.

2. *Optional:* While the paint is still damp, use a slightly darker brushload of raw sienna to create some little details.

Constructing the Luminary

1. Lay out the 4 panels and determine where you want the stars to appear. Add star cutouts to each panel, representing stars in the sky and starfish in the sea or on the beach.

2. Create 4 evenly spaced holes on both sides of each panel, making sure that each panel is exactly the same.

3. Use a length of jute twine to lash the box together. Knot the jute at the top and bottom and use a dab of clear glue to secure the knot so it does not unravel and so the knot stays outside the box, *not* hanging over the flame!

4. Hot glue seashell embellishments to the bottom corners where the panels meet.

5. Place the candle cup inside. If you're giving this as a gift, you may include my poem on a gift tag:

May the stars in the sky and the ones in the sea always twinkle in your heart and remind you of me.

Kyoto Clutch

Finished size: 15″ wide × 9¾″ tall

A traditional hand-stitching technique applied to books, Japanese stab binding is a decorative element perfect for kraft-tex. Simple yet sophisticated, this thin handbag opens up to hold your essentials. Add this statement piece to your own accessories, or gift it to someone with style.

Photo by Lindsay Hinderer

About the Maker

Artist: Lindsay Conner

Website: lindsaysews.com

See Lindsay's artist/compiler bio (page 3).

Materials

kraft-tex Basics, Vintage, or Designer:* 15˝ × 19¾˝

Hemp cord: 3½ yards, cut in half

Needles: Embroidery hand-sewing needle with a large eye

Pressing tool: Bone folder *or* Alex Anderson's 4-in-1 Essential Sewing Tool (by C&T Publishing)

* Buying prewashed kraft-tex, or prewashing it yourself, is helpful for this project.

Make It

From the Kyoto Clutch stab binding pattern (pullout page P1), prepare a template on printer paper.

Cut the kraft-tex

1. Joining the 15˝ ends together, fold the kraft-tex in half. Flatten the folded edge with a bone folder.

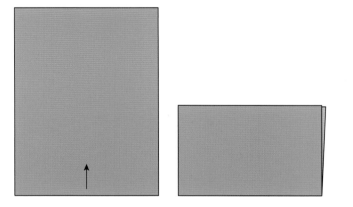

2. With the fold positioned at the bottom, measure 1¼˝ from the left side of the folded kraft-tex. Using a ruler, score with a bone folder, and fold along the line. Repeat with the right side. Flip over and repeat on the back.

3. With kraft-tex unfolded and wrong side facing up, measure 1½˝ from the top of a 15˝ edge, and 4½˝ from the left and right sides. Mark a small dot with a pencil at each point, and connect the dots. Measure 1¼˝ down from the line you just drew, and mark a dot 4½˝ from the left and right sides.

Connect the dots, drawing a box for the handle cutout. Use a ruler and craft knife to carefully cut out the handle.

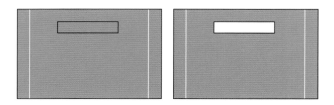

4. Fold the kraft-tex in half again, and use the hole you just made to cut out the handle on the opposite side.

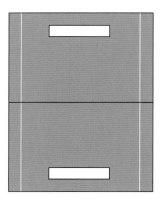

5. Clip the Kyoto Clutch Japanese stab binding pattern (pullout page P1) to the left side of the clutch, and secure with binding clips. Use a large needle to poke a hole through the center of each dot. Bring the needle all the way through, then use the tip of the craft knife to enlarge each hole so that 2 or 3 strands of hemp cord can easily fit through. Be careful not to make the holes too large—they should *not* be as large as they are on the pattern.

6. Repeat Step 5 on the right side of the clutch.

Hand Stitch the Edges

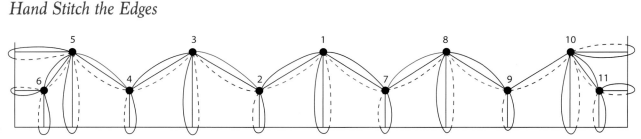

Dashed lines mean the stitch is on the other side.

1. Tie a double knot about 2″ from one end of the hemp cord.

2. Starting from the inside of the clutch, stitch up through hole 1 of the front, leaving the 2″ tail on the inside. Make a stitch over the edge of the clutch, bringing the cord back up through hole 1.

3. Make a stitch down into hole 2, and make a stitch over the edge of the clutch, going back down into hole 2 again.

4. Make a stitch up into hole 3, and make a stitch over the edge of the clutch, as you did in Step 2.

5. Make a stitch down into hole 4, and make a stitch over the edge of the clutch, as you did in Step 3.

6. Repeat Step 4 into hole 5, then make another stitch over the fold of the clutch, coming back up at hole 5.

7. Make a stitch down into hole 6, then stitch over the edge of the clutch and over the fold of the clutch, returning down into hole 6 each time.

8. Stitch from hole 6 to hole 5, then to holes 4, 3, 2, and 1, completing one half of the binding, following the red lines.

9. Make a stitch down into hole 7, and continue stitching following the pattern established in Steps 3–8, using holes 7–11 following the black lines, and then the red lines to return to the center.

10. When making the last stitch from hole 7 to hole 1, stitch only through to the inside of the clutch.

11. Tie the beginning tail of cord to the end of the cord with a knot and trim the tails to ½˝. Tuck the tails within the seam.

Detail of stitching

Boho Embroidered Bracelets

Finished size: 1″ wide × 8½″ long

Handmade bracelets are the perfect accessory to add color and fun to your outfit. Make several in coordinating colors and experiment with different designs! Colors and designs are suggested, but feel free to mix and match.

Photo by Sara Curtis

About the Maker

Artist: Sara Curtis

Website: radianthomestudio.com

Sara is a sewing pattern designer, blogger, and small business owner. She enjoys using sewing, print-making, photography, and graphic design to inspire people to notice beauty in the ordinary. Sara lives in the country with her husband and seven children, where they enjoy lots of time reading, creating, and playing outside.

Materials

kraft-tex Designer:* 4 colors (Blue Iris, Orchid, Tangerine, and Turquoise), 1 scrap 1″ × 8½″ or larger of each color

Snaps and snap tools: Size ½″

Embroidery floss: In coordinating colors

Embroidery needle

Awl or stiletto: Such as in Alex Anderson's 4-in-1 Essential Sewing Tool (by C&T Publishing)

* Reminder: These colors are hand-dyed and prewashed.

Cutting

kraft-tex: Cut 2 strips 1″ × 8½″ for each bracelet.

Note: Adjust the Size

Small adjustments to the finished size can be made by changing the snap placement. To custom fit the bracelet to your wrist, measure around your wrist without any ease, then add 1¾″ to the length.

Make It

Stitch the Embroidery

1. Choose an embroidery stitch diagram and prepare a template for your chosen Boho Embroidery Bracelets pattern (page 106). Secure it to the top of a strip of kraft-tex with sewing clips. Use an awl to poke holes through each dot, piercing through the paper and kraft-tex.

2. Remove the paper and stitch the design (following the individual instructions on pages 24 and 25) onto the top layer of kraft-tex. Stitch one color at a time, making knots on the back as needed. Be sure not to skip across the back to a hole that is more than 1″ away.

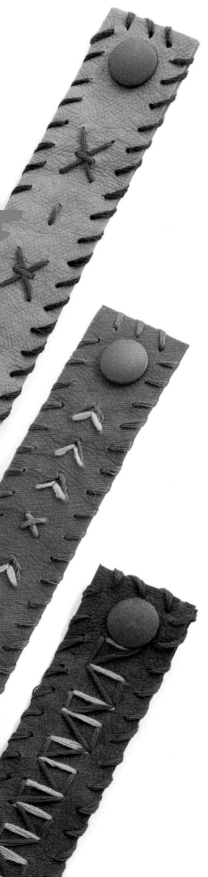

DESIGN 1 (TURQUOISE)

1. Stitch the 5 orange X's by stitching up through the outer corners and in through the center hole.

2. Stitch across the first orange X with teal, then make the short stitch between the X's.

3. Alternate these stitches to the end of the bracelet.

4. See Finish the Bracelet (next page). Whipstitch the edges with olive green.

DESIGN 2 (TANGERINE)

1. Stitch the 4 sets of 3 teal arrows.

2. Stitch the 4 sets of 3 white arrows, using the same holes for the bottoms of the arrows.

3. Stitch the 3 small X's with turquoise.

4. See Finish the Bracelet (next page). Whipstitch the edges with teal.

DESIGN 3 (BLUE IRIS)

1. Use a running stitch to stitch 2 vertical parallel lines of light purple down the bracelet. Make sure the parallel lines are opposite, so that when a stitch is on top on the left, the parallel stitch on the right is on the bottom. There will be 2 open holes, one on each end.

2. Using the same holes, use a running stitch to stitch horizontal stripes with white. The horizontal stripes will fill the empty holes on the ends.

3. Using the same holes again, stitch a zigzag backstitch with orange.

4. See Finish the Bracelet (below). Whipstitch the edges with orange.

DESIGN 4 (ORCHID)

1. Stitch the 4 white X's, stitching up through the outer corners and in through the center hole.

2. Stitch the red and dark purple horizontal lines. These do not cross over each other. They will be pulled together by the center stitch.

3. Use orange to pull together the purple horizontal lines. Push the needle up through the center hole and come up on the outside of an outside line. Wrap the floss around all 3 lines and go back down through the same hole, pulling tight and knotting the thread on the back.

4. Repeat Step 3, using dark purple to pull together the orange horizontal lines and to cross over the white X's from Step 1.

5. See Finish the Bracelet (below). Whipstitch the edges with dark purple.

Finish the Bracelet

1. Align and secure the second strip of kraft-tex to the back of the first, using sewing clips. Use an awl to mark holes along the edge of the bracelet ¼″ apart and ⅛″ from the edge. Whipstitch around the edges, using a piece of embroidery floss about 40″ long, hiding the knots between the layers.

2. Add snaps, following the manufacturer's directions. If needed, make small adjustments to the snap placement to change the finished size of the bracelet.

Pretty Vase Sleeves

Finished sizes: 8⅛˝ wide × 4˝ tall
10˝ wide × 5½˝ tall • 13½˝ wide × 7⅞˝ tall

Upcycle tin cans and glass jars into something beautiful, using white kraft-tex and your prettiest bits of lace, buttons, and more! Use the containers as vases to hold fresh-cut flowers from the garden, or to stash pens, pencils, or other art supplies. The sizes I made fit to wrap around a 6-ounce tomato paste can, a 16-ounce jam jar, or a 28-ounce bean can. You could also wrap existing vases to match your decor.

Photo by Magdalena Lindner

About the Maker

Artist: Kristyne Czepuryk

Website: prettybyhand.com

Kristyne is a lifelong crafter who loves making pretty things. Her favorite childhood gifts were always kits—the ones filled with supplies, tools, and colorful project booklets. Although she still loves the creative process of making, she enjoys inspiring other makers even more. She is the author of *S Is for Stitch* (by Stash Books).

tips

Use a heat-sensitive, temporary pen (such as a FriXion pen, by Pilot) and a ruler to draw straight horizontal lines to help position objects evenly.

Punch tiny holes with an awl or stiletto to help position buttonholes and embroidery stitches accurately.

Materials

kraft-tex Basics or Vintage— White: ½ yard is enough to make all 3 sizes shown

Used glass jars or tin cans: Various sizes

Decorative scissors

Measuring tape

White glue

Decorative objects: Such as lace, ribbon, trims, buttons, string, and twine

Embroidery floss

Embroidery needle

Awl or stiletto: Such as in Alex Anderson's 4-in-1 Essential Sewing Tool (by C&T Publishing)

Cutting

Measure the height and circumference of the container. Cut a rectangle of kraft-tex ½˝ longer than the circumference and ½˝ taller than desired height.

Make It

1. Use decorative scissors to trim the top edge of the kraft-tex.

2. Place decorative objects on the kraft-tex in a pleasing arrangement. Take a photo of the desired layout.

3. Remove the objects and attach the bottom-layer objects first, using white glue or a sewing machine.

4. Add additional objects, attaching with stitching or glue.

5. Trim 1 vertical edge with decorative ribbon, trim, or an extra strip of kraft-tex.

6. Spread glue on the back of the sleeve, and wrap the sleeve around the container, ensuring the decorative trim is on the outside to cover the opposite raw edge. Wrap the string around the sleeve to hold it in place until the glue dries. Remove the string.

7. *Optional:* Wrap with some additional decorative ribbon or twine, or you can even omit the glue and simply tie the sleeve around the container. Then the sleeve is removable and can be stored flat.

Meditation Flags

Finished size (each flag): 3¾″ wide × 4″ tall

A string of meditation flags add a touch of homemade decor. Printed with various emblems for relaxation, this quick project is easy to customize to your own personal style. These emblems, depicting elements of the earth, can be substituted by anything that makes you happy.

Photo by Kent Ratliff

About the Maker

Artist: Karen Ratliff

Instagram: @quilted_escapades

Using her hands to create has always been part of Karen's life. Her creative outlets include crafting, sewing, quilting, and home improvement. She and her husband recently finished installing wood floors throughout their house. Her husband always deferred the "special cuts" to her because of how close they were to piecing a quilt. She lives in Greenwood, Indiana.

Materials

kraft-tex Basics or Vintage—White: ¼ yard or more, depending on size and number of flags

Jute string: 3 yards

Gel printing plate

Fabric paint or ink

Brayer

Textured objects: Such as stamps, stickers, combs, or stencils to create designs

Fabric markers

Glue (*optional*): You can also use a sewing machine.

Cutting

Cut kraft-tex the same size as the gel printing plate.

Make It

1. Add paint to the gel printing plate and use a brayer to roll a thin layer of paint on the plate. Place the kraft-tex on the plate and apply pressure to transfer paint.

2. Remove the kraft-tex and allow the paint to dry.

3. Use the brayer to add another layer of paint to the plate, and use a texture object of your choice to create a pattern. Remove the kraft-tex, and allow it to dry.

4. Cut the printed kraft-tex into desired number of flags. (I cut 7 pieces 3¾˝ × 4½˝.)

5. Add a focal point emblem using stamps, stickers, or hand drawing. (I used a fabric marker and drew the emblems based on designs I found that represented elements of the earth.) If you want your design to be centered in the end, be sure to account for the ½˝ fold (you'll see in Step 7).

6. Make 6 more flags in this manner (or as many as desired).

7. Fold the top of each flag ½˝ down and insert the jute within the fold. Use a clip to hold it in place, and glue or sew the jute string inside the sleeve. Repeat for all flags, leaving an inch or more between each flag.

Celestial Coasters

Finished size: 7″ wide × 7⅜″ tall

Practice English paper piecing these starry drink coasters to dress up your table. With a sturdy kraft-tex bottom and your cotton fabric, this quick idea is great for scraps left over from other projects.

Photo by Stephanie Woodson

About the Maker

Artist: Stephanie Woodson

Website: swoodsonsays.com

Stephanie is a blogger who loves trying everything creative. Sewing keeps her sane while she wrangles her two young kids. Some of her passions are embroidering, using up fabric scraps, making handmade softies, and working with upcycled materials.

Materials

kraft-tex Designer:

- **Blue Iris:** ¼ yard
- **Orchid:** ¼ yard

Quilting cotton squares: 1 charm pack or 10 large scraps

Hand sewing needles

Coordinating thread

Glue stick

Card stock: To make the template

Air-soluble marking pen

Cutting

From the Celestial Coasters pattern (page 111), prepare a diamond template.

kraft-tex: Cut 1 piece 7½″ × 7½″ for each coaster.

Card stock: Cut 5 diamonds for each coaster.

Make It

1. Apply a dab of glue stick to the back of a card stock diamond and lightly stick it to the wrong side of the fabric. Make sure there is roughly ¼″ seam allowance around all edges, and then cut around it. Use your nail or a finger-press tool to firmly fold the fabric back over the edges of the template, one side at a time.

Instructional photos by Stephanie Woodson

2. Thread a needle and take small stitches to secure each corner around the template, making sure not to sew through the paper or the front of the shape. Press the diamond.

3. Thread a needle and make small stitches in between 2 diamonds, right sides together, along adjacent edges. Use a whipstitch and stitch right along the edges. Repeat until all 5 diamonds have formed a star.

Instructional photos by Stephanie Woodson

4. Fold the overhanging fabric from the top of each diamond straight down, and take 1 or 2 stitches to tack it down through the seam allowance fabric at each star point, being careful not to stitch through the front or the card stock.

5. Use an iron to press the entire star, and press flat the remaining hanging fabric at the middle of the star. Gently remove the papers and press again.

6. Use a glue stick around the wrong sides of the star and adhere it to the 7½″ × 7½″ square of kraft-tex. Hand sew or machine sew the paper-pieced star onto the kraft-tex, ⅛″ from the edge.

7. Use an acrylic quilt ruler and trace around each edge ½˝ from the fabric star edges. Carefully cut the kraft-tex star along this line.

Projects

After you've gotten cozy with kraft-tex, you're ready to dive in! Sew twelve projects from wallets and purses to thoughtful handmade gifts and stylish accessories. With a wide variety of surface design treatments, you'll get your hands wet with embroidery, cutting, printing, painting, and more! The detailed instructions will help you step up your kraft-tex game as you construct impressive shapes, install bag hardware, and try out new assembly.

Modern Art Necklace

Finished size: 7½″ diameter

kraft-tex is the perfect medium for jewelry—durable and allergy-free. This modern necklace is easy to make and lends itself to your artistic design interpretation. No matter what colors you choose, you're sure to make a bold statement, leaving your friends guessing which fancy boutique this necklace is from.

Photo by Odd Anders Brevik

About the Maker

Artist: Normajean Brevik

Blog: seasew.blogspot.com

See Normajean's artist bio
(page 15).

tip

Easy-to-cut abstract and
organic shapes work well. Dots
or punches in different sizes
add a bit of serendipity, and
steel edge punches can add
panache and set a theme.

Materials

kraft-tex Basics, Vintage, or Designer: * 2 colors,
10″ × 13″ of each color

Steel-edge paper punches: Including ⅟₁₆″, ⅛″,
and ¼″ round-hole punches

Hook-and-loop tape: 1″ piece

Clear-drying permanent glue

Heavy card stock: To make the template

*Buying prewashed kraft-tex, or prewashing it yourself,
is helpful for this project.*

Cutting

*From the Modern Art Necklace pattern (pullout page P1),
prepare a template on heavy card stock. Read though the
cutting directions carefully before beginning.*

1. Try on the necklace template and make any necessary
adjustments to fit properly. If adjustments are needed, make
a second template to try on.

2. Trace the template to the *wrong side* of the kraft-tex
bottom layer (whichever color of kraft-tex you want on the
bottom of your necklace) and cut it out with scissors or craft
knife. *Note:* This is the only side that you use the template for.

3. Place the top layer piece of kraft-tex *right side down*, with
the previously cut bottom layer piece *right side down* on
top, and trace an outline. *Note:* Because it is a tracing, it will
be slightly larger; you will trim it later. This helps cover and
eliminate any tiny irregularities from your first cut.

Make It

Create Decorative Cutouts

1. Sketch design layout ideas on a tracing of the pattern.
Be sure not to set design choices too close to the edge,
since you will be trimming and stitching the 2 layers
together and must leave room for the stitch line.

2. Once you are happy with your sketched designs, audition them. Use the original card stock template, transfer the designs, and cut them out.

3. Use this design template like a stencil, penciling your designs onto the right side of the kraft-tex on the *top layer only*.

4. Punch or cut out the design holes.

Join the Top and Bottom Layers

1. Place tiny dots of glue on the wrong side of the *top layer*, being careful not to get too close to the design holes. Press the 2 pieces together. Lay flat and cover with a piece of wax or parchment paper, weigh down with a book, and let set until dry.

2. Very carefully, trim the top and bottom layer evenly.

3. Carefully and *slowly* stitch the top and bottom together, stitching about ³⁄₁₆″ away from the edge around the entire piece. If helpful, use clips to keep any unglued areas from shifting while sewing. I find it helpful to use an open-toe foot and the needle-down mode.

Attach the Hook-and-Loop Tape

1. Temporarily attach the looped soft side of the hook-and-loop tape to the back/wrong side of the wider end of the necklace.

2. Temporarily attach the hooked rough side of the hook-and-loop tape to the front/right side of the narrower end of the necklace.

3. Determine the best wearing angle position for your hook-and-loop tape and glue each piece in place. Let it dry flat with the tape separated and weighed down with books.

Journal Necklace

Finished sizes:

Journal: 1¼″ wide × 1⅝″ tall × ¼″ deep • Necklace: 16″ long

This sweet journal necklace may be too small to hold your deep thoughts, but it's the perfect handmade accessory. Choose neutral colors, or go bold with brights—the choice is yours! Add shiny or antique charms and a metal chain to finish the look. These tiny books make perfect friendship necklaces for your besties.

Photo by Lindsay Hinderer

About the Maker

Artist: Lindsay Conner

Website: lindsaysews.com

See Lindsay's artist/compiler bio (page 3).

Materials

kraft-tex Basics, Vintage, or Designer: Scraps at least 1⅝″ × 2¾″ for journal cover

White construction paper: 1 sheet 9″ × 12″ (or 2 sheets to make 3 journals)

White thread

Embroidery floss

Hand-sewing needles: Large and small eye

Metal chain: 28″ long

Jewelry pliers

Split jump rings: 2 or 3

Hemp cord (*optional*)

Metal charms and keys (*optional*): For embellishment

Spring ring clasp (*optional*)

Make It

Stitch the Journal

1. Fold and tear each sheet of construction paper according to the journal-page tearing diagram. Each sheet yields 32 pieces 1½″ × 2¼″, and you will use 18 per journal.

Journal-page tearing

2. Join 3 pages into a signature by folding them horizontally into a small book and stitching them together with white thread and a small hand-sewing needle, as shown. Make 6 signatures per journal.

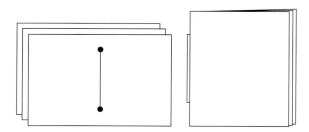

3. Fold the journal cover around the signatures. Secure with a binding clip.

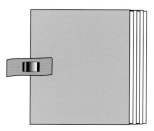

4. Using 3 strands of embroidery floss, stitch an embroidery design of your choice (for example, X's, zigzags, argyle) through the spine of the journal, catching the pages as you go. Stitch between each folded signature 1 or 2 times until the book is secure.

5. Leave the book open or secure it using one of the following options:

- *Tie a piece of kraft-tex around it:* Cut a small strand ⅛″ wide and tie a single knot.

- *Secure with hemp cord:* Make a hole in the cover as shown, and tie a knot through the cord on the inside of the book. Wrap it around the book twice and secure the other end with a metal key or embellishment.

Hemp cord option: Poke hole in cover for cord.

Finish the Necklace

1. Use a large embroidery needle to poke a hole in the top of the journal as shown. Open and insert a jump ring, using jewelry pliers.

2. Attach this ring to the ends of the metal chain, and close; *or* if using a spring ring clasp, insert the journal's ring onto the middle of the chain, and the clasp on both ends. The necklace is long enough to slip over your head even without a clasp.

3. Attach charms with additional jump rings if desired.

Magnetic Fridge Organizer

Finished size: 8″ wide × 19¾″ tall

This handy organizer can be used on a fridge, locker, or any magnetic surface to keep small papers organized. Keep a pen ready in the loop at the top and hang a spiral notepad from the bottom! You'll also practice weaving and flower-making with kraft-tex.

Photo by Sara Curtis

About the Maker

Artist: Sara Curtis

Website: radianthomestudio.com

See Sara's artist bio (page 23).

Materials

kraft-tex Basics—Natural: 1 roll

kraft-tex Designer:

• **Tangerine:** 1 sheet

• **Blue Iris:** 1 sheet

Magnets: 6 strong magnets, ½″–¾″ round

Removable tape: Such as washi tape

Tacky glue

Coordinating thread

Cutting

From the Magnetic Fridge Organizer patterns (page 107), prepare the flower and circle templates.

From Natural kraft-tex, cut:

• 2 pieces 8″ × 19¾″ for front and back

• 1 piece 8″ × 4½″ for upper pocket

• 1 piece 10½″ × 8″ for lower pocket

• 6 squares 2″ × 2″ to cover magnets

From Tangerine kraft-tex, cut:

• 2 pieces 8″ × 1″ for notepad holder

• 2 strips 11″ × ¼″ strip for weaving

• 1 strip 11″ × ½″ strip for weaving

• 1 small flower from the template

From Blue Iris kraft-tex, cut:

• 1 piece ½″ × 8″ for upper pocket edge

• 1 piece 1″ × 8″ for lower pocket edge

• 1 piece 1″ × 2½″ for pen loop

• Several ¼″-wide strips cut into 3″ lengths (about 40 total 3″ strips)

• 1 large flower from the template

• 1 circle from the template

Make It

Prepare the Embellishments

WEAVE THE BOTTOM POCKET EMBELLISHMENT

1. Tape the 3 Tangerine strips on a table with the ½″ strip in the center. Weave the 3″ Blue Iris strips over and under, alternating as you go. Push the strips together as tightly as possible, taping the Blue Iris strips as needed to keep everything together.

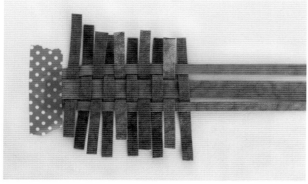

Instructional photo by Sara Curtis

2. Machine stitch above and below the edges of the weaving, about ⅛″ away from the Tangerine strips and remove the tape. Trim woven strips ⅛″ outside the stitching. The final strip width is about 1¾″. Set aside.

PREPARE THE FLOWERS

1. Layer the pieces cut from templates, with the small flower on top of the large one, and with the small circle centered on top, to make the flower unit.

2. Stitch 2 free-motion circles around the edge of the small circle.

3. Place the flower unit on the upper pocket piece about 1½″ from the upper left corner.

Stitch 3 lines across the center of the circle, creating an asterisk shape through all the flower layers and the pocket. Set aside.

Construct the Front

1. Align the 2 Tangerine strips 8″ × 1″ for the notepad holder. Machine stitch the long edges about ⅛″ from the edge. Set aside.

2. On the lower pocket piece, measure 1½″ from the 8″ sides. Score and fold the flaps toward the back. Measure ¾″ from the 8″ sides, and score and fold the flaps toward the front. You should have about ¼″ of material showing beyond the fold on each side with a total width of 8″ when folded.

3. Place the woven strip on the lower pocket 1″ below the top edge. Unfold the pocket flaps and stitch through the woven strip and pocket ⅛″ inside the first row of stitching on the woven strip. Trim the edges even with the pocket sides. Refold the pocket flaps.

4. Glue baste or clip the edges of the pockets in place as you attach them to the back piece. Align the top of the upper pocket 2″ from the top of 1 back piece. Place the ½″ Blue Iris strip centered over the bottom edge of the upper pocket. Edge stitch the long edges of the strip at the bottom of the upper pocket.

5. Align the top of the lower pocket 8″ from the top of the front piece. Place the 1″ Blue Iris strip centered over the bottom edge of the lower pocket. Edge stitch the long edges of the strip at the bottom of the lower pocket, making sure to keep the flaps folded under and aligned with the sides. Stitch slowly through the thick layers.

6. Align the Tangerine notepad holder 1⅛″ from the bottom of the front piece, and glue baste or

clip in place. Align the pen loop at the top center edge and glue baste or clip in place. Set aside the entire front piece and pockets.

Construct the Back

1. Glue each of the 6 magnets on the wrong side of the back piece about ½˝ from the edges (one in each corner and one centered on each long side).

2. Place the 2˝ × 2˝ squares over each magnet. Edge stitch the 2 inside edges of each square of the corner magnets, and edgestitch the 3 inside edges of each square on the side magnets. (The remaining loose edges will be caught in the final stitching around the entire organizer.)

Finish the Organizer

1. Align the front and the back, carefully matching all edges. Trim and make adjustments, if necessary.

2. Slowly edge stitch around the entire rectangle at ⅛˝, making sure to stitch over the pocket sides, pen loop, and notebook holder.

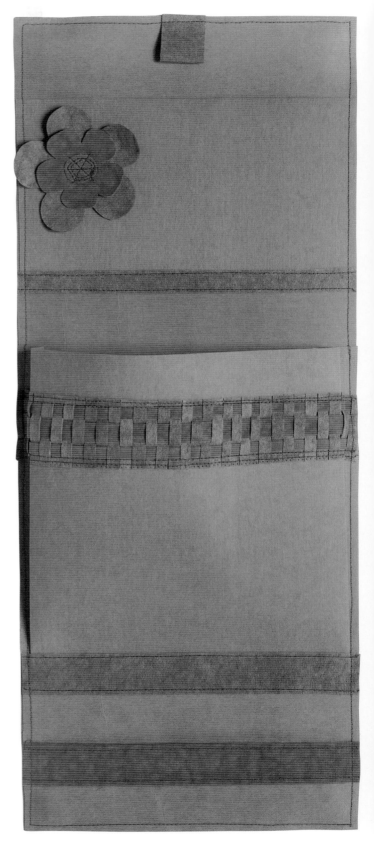

Rainbow Crossbody Bag

Finished size: 9″ wide × 6½″ tall × 2½″ deep

Put your kraft-tex skills to the test! This project is ideal for kraft-tex aficionados, with special dyeing techniques, bag hardware, and tips for turning and shaping kraft-tex. With inner dividers to keep you organized, this fully lined bag is one you'll be proud to use every day.

Photo by Nissa Brehmer

About the Maker

Artist: Mary E. Flynn

Instagram: @maryelf

Mary is a Brooklyn-born, Bay Area–based quiltmaker and designer (and mother of two adult children) who has recently ventured into bag design. Like so many others, she learned sewing at home from her mother.

Materials

kraft-tex Basics or Vintage—White:* At least 18½″ × 28½″

Foam stabilizer: 20″ wide (sew-in or fusible), ¾ yard

Woven fusible interfacing: 20″ wide
(such as Shape-Flex by Pellon), ¾ yard

Cotton fabric: 40″ wide, ¾ yard, for bag lining

Utility nylon underlining: 58″ wide, ¼ yard

Zippers:

- *Metal:* 2, 12″ long, for zip compartment tops
- *Nylon coil:* 7″ long for zip pocket

Magnetic snaps: 2, ¾″ diameter, for center compartment

Rectangle rings: 2, ¾″ diameter

Rectangle slider: ¾″ size

Coordinating thread

* Buying prewashed kraft-tex, or prewashing it yourself, is helpful for this project.

Tools and Supplies

Fabric paints: Such as Jacquard Dye-Na-Flow or Marabu Textil

Perle cotton #5 or #8: Or other means of tying folds in place

Bone folder or pressing tool: Such as in Alex Anderson's 4-in-1 Essential Sewing Tool (by C&T Publishing)

Washable wonder tape

Fabric clips: Such as Clover Wonder Clips, or binder clips

Awl or stiletto: Such as in Alex Anderson's 4-in-1 Essential Sewing Tool

Seam roller: Or clean brayer

Metal turning tool: With ball at the end (such as Precision Turning Tool, by RNK Distributing)

Paint-safe dish

Quarter: To trace for corner curves

Cutting

From the Rainbow Crossbody Bag patterns (pullout page P2), prepare templates for the bag front and back, snap panel, sides/bottom, inner zipper compartment (front and back), center compartment bottom A and B, slip pocket, and zipper pocket. Color the kraft-tex before cutting.

kraft-tex

• Cut 2 bag front and back.

• Cut 2 snap panels.

• Cut 1 sides/bottom.

• Cut 2 rectangles ¾˝ × 2½˝ for the strap anchors.

• Cut 7 rectangles ¾˝ × 18½˝ for strap.

Foam

• Cut 2 bag front and back.

• Cut 2 inner zipper compartment.

Utility nylon

• Cut 2 bag front and back.

• Cut 2 snap panels.

• Cut 1 sides/bottom.

• Cut 2 rectangles ¾˝ × 2½˝ for the strap anchors.

• Cut 1 rectangle ⅝˝ × 58˝ for strap.

• Cut 7 squares ¾˝ × ¾˝ for joining the strap pieces.

Woven fusible interfacing

• Cut 1 sides/bottom.

• Cut 1 center compartment bottom, side A.

• Cut 1 center compartment bottom, side B.

> **tip**
>
> Fuse a large piece of woven fusible interfacing to the lining fabric first, then cut out the fused units.

Lining fabric

• Cut 2 bag front and back.

• Cut 1 sides/bottom.

• Cut 2 inner zipper compartment.

• Cut 1 center compartment bottom, side A.

• Cut 1 center compartment bottom, side B.

• Cut 1 slip pocket.

• Cut 1 zipper pocket.

• Cut 4 squares 1½˝ × 1½˝ for the zipper end tabs.

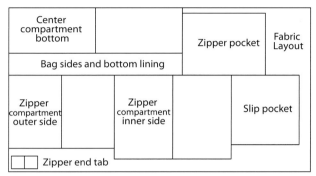

Lining fabric cutting layout

Color the kraft-tex

1. Soak the kraft-tex in water, then crinkle and squish it. Hold it up to light: if it has a nice two-tone crinkle pattern throughout, it's ready. Let it drip dry for a bit, then roll it in a towel to eliminate drips.

2. Using a quilting ruler and a bone folder or ruler, score evenly spaced, horizontal lines about 1˝ apart across the entire surface. Fold the kraft-tex along the score lines using a bone folder or ruler.

3. Turn the kraft-tex over and fold the creases back on themselves. Use the bone folder to impress the crease in the opposite direction for all creased lines.

4. Arrange folds accordion-style across the entire piece. The kraft-tex is likely to resist such manipulation. Be firm.

5. Secure the pleats at one end with a rubber band around all folds.

6. Beginning at the other end, use perle cotton to wrap around the folds several times, then move over about 1″ and wrap again. Continue wrapping and moving until you have wrapped the entire length along the folds. Remove the rubber band and secure the string.

tip

Because kraft-tex dries fairly quickly, you may want to re-wet it before beginning the coloring process.

7. Count the number of spaces in your tied-off bundle. Decide how many colors you want in your shibori dyeing, and where you want each color to go.

8. Place the tied bundle on a protected work surface. Add a small amount of dye into a paint-safe dish. Use a brush and apply color to the folded edges on the top and bottom of all the spaces designated for that color. Add the dye in sections, continuing across the bundle until you have used all the colors you chose.

tip

When you apply the color, it will spread beyond your tied areas. Don't worry—just continue to apply colors in order, and let them blend.

9. When you're done, cut and unwind the string, unfold the finished piece, and hang it to dry.

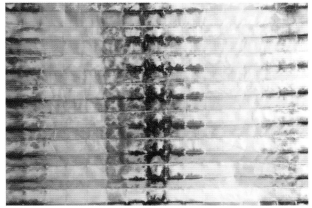

Instructional photo by Mary E. Flynn

10. Press the finished kraft-tex on both sides to heat-set the color and flatten it for cutting.

Prepare to Sew

Underlining

Attach nylon pieces to the wrong side of the kraft-tex pieces using glue or spray adhesive.

Fusing

1. Fuse foam pieces (or sew in) to the back of designated fabric pieces.

2. Fuse woven fusible interfacing pieces to the back of designated fabric pieces.

Transferring Markings

1. Transfer the dot and pleat markings from the templates to the snap panels, sides/bottom, and slip pocket. Transfer the snap placement markings to the snap panels.

2. Mark the vertical centers at the top and bottom of all pieces.

Shaping

For the kraft-tex bag front and back pieces, place a quarter at the bottom corners. Trace the curve into the corner, and cut around the curves.

Initial Sewing

All seam allowances are ¼˝.

Make and Attach Zipper End Tabs

1. Turn under one side of each zipper end tab ¼˝.

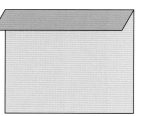

2. Place them right sides together with folded edges together.

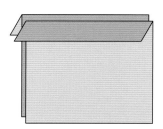

3. Sew 3 unfolded sides, backstitching at the beginning and end.

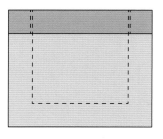

4. Turn right side out.

5. Tuck the ends of the 12˝ zippers inside.

6. Edgestitch across the open end adjacent to the zipper stop and around the whole tab.

7. *Optional:* Use 1˝ × 1˝ squares of kraft-tex. Lay the squares next to the zipper stop on the top and bottom, and edgestitch across the zipper bottom and around all 4 sides, enclosing the zipper tape.

Make Strap Anchors

1. Edgestitch along both long edges of each strap anchor, with the nylon piece already glued to the back.

2. Slide each strap anchor through a rectangle ring, and baste the short ends together.

3. Baste the strap anchors in place, centered on the short ends of the sides/bottom, raw edges aligned.

Magnetic Snap Placement

Follow the manufacturer's directions to install snaps, 2 males on snap panel A and 2 females on snap panel B.

Install 2 male snaps on snap panel A.

Install 2 female snaps on snap panel B.

Make the Slip Pocket

1. Fold the slip pocket in half, right sides together, and stitch around 3 sides, leaving an opening on the bottom. Clip the corners.

2. Turn right side out, folding the allowances on the unstitched opening to inside along the seamline. Press.

3. Edgestitch along the upper folded edge.

4. Bring the dots on the bottom edge together to form pocket pleats.

5. Clip the pleats in place. Clip the opening closed.

Attach the Slip Pocket

1. Place the slip pocket on the center compartment bottom A along the markings from the template, centered vertically and 1″ up from the lower raw edge.

2. Edgestitch in place along 3 sides, stitching over pleats and closing the opening to finish the center compartment bottom A.

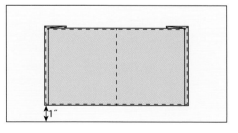

3. *Optional:* Stitch through the center of pocket, creating 2 pockets.

Make Zipper Pocket

1. Transfer the rectangle guide marking on the template to the wrong side of the zipper pocket. The rectangle is 7″ × ½″, centered vertically with its upper edge ¾″ down from the pocket's upper edge.

2. Place the zipper pocket and the center compartment bottom B right sides together, aligning the upper raw edges and center marks.

3. Stitch around the rectangle marking.

4. Make a long slit in the center of the stitched rectangle for the pocket, and cut into the corners. Snip right up to, but not through, the corner stitches.

5. Turn the pocket through the opening and press the seam.

6. Pin the pieces together.

Sew Zipper in Place

1. Place the zipper under the opening, centered horizontally and with the zipper pull at the left side of the opening. Use pins or washable wonder tape to hold the zipper in place.

2. Edgestitch the zipper in place around the opening.

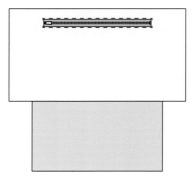

Finish Zipper Pocket

1. Fold the zipper pocket along the fold line, right sides together, aligning all raw edges at the top.

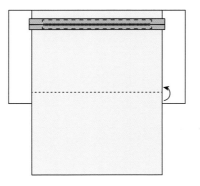

2. Move the sides of the center compartment bottom out of the way, and sew the right and left seams of the zipper pocket from the fold up to the top.

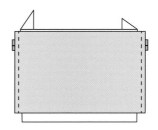

3. Baste through all the layers along the upper raw edges within the seam allowance.

Make the Straps

1. Place the strap pieces end to end. Place ¾″ × ¾″ nylon squares beneath joins, and stitch back and forth several times through all layers.

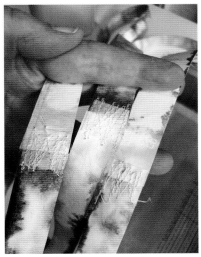

Instructional photo by Mary E. Flynn

2. Trim the strap to 116″, then sew the ends together with the ¾″ × ¾″ nylon square beneath, forming a loop.

3. Fold the strap loop flat, adjusting it until all joints lie in different locations so that none are on top of another.

4. Place the ⅝″ × 58″ nylon underlining inside the loop and lightly glue to one side.

5. Topstitch and edgestitch along both long edges.

Bag Construction

Make Center Compartment Units A and B

1. Align the center markings and sew snap panel A to center compartment bottom A. This makes center compartment unit A.

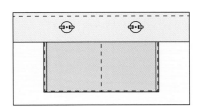

Center compartment unit A

2. Repeat Step 1 for snap panel B and center compartment bottom B to make center compartment unit B.

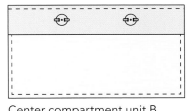

Center compartment unit B

3. Press the seam allowances up, and edgestitch on the snap panels for units A and B.

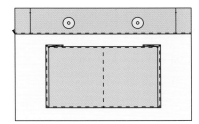

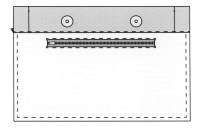

tip

Finger-press kraft-tex along the seamline, then press with a bone folder or seam roller.

Insert Zipper Half for Compartment Fronts A and B

1. Place a 12″ zipper between the foam-backed inner compartment front and center compartment unit A. Position the zipper pull to the right with the top of pull to the left of the dot and facedown onto center compartment unit A.

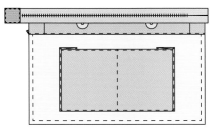

2. Place the Inner compartment front on top, facedown. Clip in place. The zippers are longer than the seams, so you can open them completely—no need to stop and slide the zipper pull in the middle of the zipper insertion!

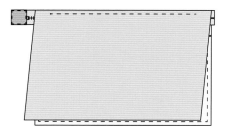

3. Stitch through all 3 layers between the dots. This makes center compartment front A.

4. Repeat Steps 1–3 for the second 12″ zipper to make center compartment front B—*but* position the zipper pull to the left with the top of the pull to the right of dot and facedown onto center compartment unit B.

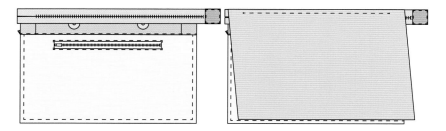

5. For both center compartment units, open the seams. Press the seam allowances away from the zipper teeth; the zipper will stick up between the layers. Edgestitch close to each zipper between the dots.

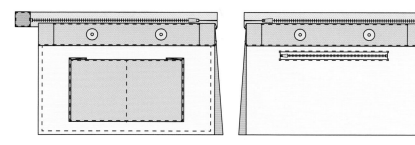

Shape Compartment Pockets

1. Fold the lower corners of the center compartment units and Inner compartment fronts diagonally by aligning sides and bottom, right sides together. For the boxed corners, mark a ¾″ stitching line 1″ away from the point of the fold that begins at the fold and ends ¼″ away from the raw edge.

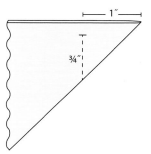

2. Stitch and backstitch on the marked lines. Open the seam allowances. Snip into the seam allowance on the fold, being sure not to clip the stitch line, so that it will open fully and lie flat.

3. For both compartment units, align the raw edges of all 3 sides, wrong sides together. Fold the snap panels on the fold line. Align the stitched

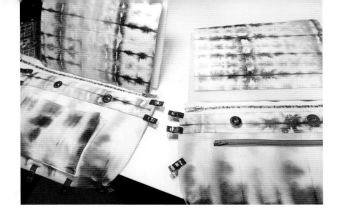

corners and push the inner compartment front corners into the center compartment unit corners to create a three-dimensional compartment.

4. Use a clip to fasten together the seam allowances of compartment unit A exterior and lining, or baste them together within the seam allowance. Repeat for compartment unit B.

Insert Zipper Half for Exterior Bag A and B

1. Beginning with center compartment unit A, layer together the foam-backed inner compartment back, the unsewn side of zipper tape, and the exterior bag. Clip in place, matching the centers of the bag pieces and aligning their upper edges with the long edge of the zipper tape. Stitch through all 3 layers between dots.

2. Repeat Step 1 for center compartment unit B and exterior bag.

3. For both compartment/exterior units: Open the seams. Press the seam allowances away from the zipper teeth. The zipper will stick up between the layers. Topstitch close to the zipper between the dots.

4. Move the exterior bag away from the inner compartment back. Align the basted edges of the corner-stitched inner front/center compartments to the raw edges of the inner compartment back, and clip or baste it in place. Match the open corners of the compartment unit to the lower corners of the Inner compartment front.

Instructional photos by Mary E. Flynn

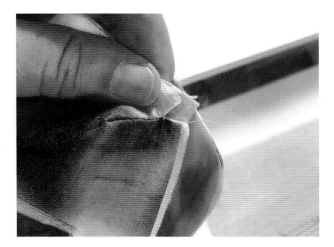

5. Beginning at the dot, stitch the seam from the top right of center compartment unit A down right side to the open corner at the lower right, keeping the seam allowances and zipper tape clear of stitching. Backstitch both ends of the seam.

6. Stitch the seam from open bottom left corner up left side to top left of center compartment unit, ending at dot. Backstitch both ends of seam. End sewing at dot, keeping seam allowances and zipper tape clear of stitching.

Instructional photos by Mary E. Flynn

7. Stitch seam across the bottom from the right corner to left corner. Backstitch both ends of the seam.

8. Repeat Steps 4–8 for second compartment/ exterior unit.

9. For both compartment units, tuck the ends of the zipper tape near the pull into the compartment.

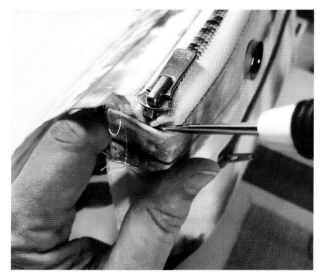

10. For both compartment units, open the zipper and flatten the unit as best you can. Topstitch, catching the zipper tape ends, continuing the line you had previously ended at the dots, in Step 6. The closed ends of the zippers with end tabs can be tucked into the purse.

Join Bag Sides/Bottom to Center Compartment Units

When sewing the bag sides/bottom to the compartments and exteriors, sew fabric to fabric and kraft-tex to kraft-tex. For bag sides/bottom lining, staystitch just inside seam allowance before and after corner dots to reinforce the corners. Snip to, not through, the dots.

1. Match the snipped corners of one side of the bag sides/bottom lining to the unsewn corners of compartment unit B that is already sewn to inner compartment back. Clip in place.

2. Clip the remainder of the bag sides/bottom lining to compartment unit B around 3 sides. Stitch all around, pivoting at the corners.

3. Clip the kraft-tex bag sides/bottom to the center compartment unit A on 3 sides; leave the corners loose.

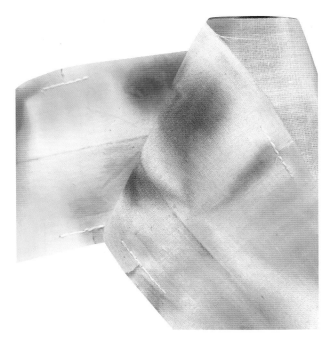

4. With sharp, pointed scissors, make a few *shallow* snips on both sides of the corner snip. Don't snip past the seam allowance! Repeat for the second corner.

5. Ease the snipped edge of the kraft-tex bag sides/bottom to the rounded corner edge of the exterior bag. Clip in place. Repeat for the second corner.

6. Stitch around all 3 sides.

7. At the beginning and end of the stitching line, sew all the way to the top of the exterior bag, ignoring those dots.

8. After the seam is complete, return to the corners and sew a reinforcement seam close to the original seamline within the seam allowances. Begin and end near the corner easing snips.

9. On the exterior bag at both corners, make notches to reduce bulk.

Join Bag Halves

1. Arrange 2 bag halves as shown.

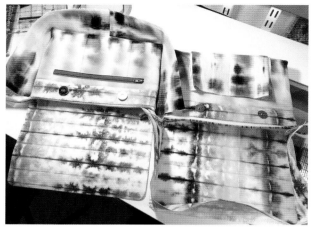

Instructional photo by Mary E. Flynn

2. Flip half over the other half, allowing compartments A and B to face each other and the snaps to connect.

3. Repeat the steps in Join Bag Sides/Bottom to Center Compartment Units (page 59), but don't sew the bottom center seam as in Step 2. This will remain open for turning. Backstitch at the beginning and end of side seams.

4. Place half of the bag into the other half of the bag, wrong sides out. It's not important which half is which.

5. Open the seam allowances at the tops of seams between the bag sides/bottom and the exterior bag.

6. Wrong sides still out, clip together the short ends of the bag sides/bottom—kraft-tex side and lining side—keeping those seam allowances open.

7. Stitch the opening from one side to the other, beginning and ending at the seam allowances. Catch the raw edges of strap anchors in the seam.

Turn Bag to Right Side

1. Turn the bag right side out through opening in the bag lining bottom. Use a turning tool to help open up the seams.

2. Sew the opening in the bag lining closed, then turn it to the inside.

3. Pull the strap anchors all the way up, and finger-press the seam allowances of upper bag sides/bottom. Massage everything else into place.

Attach Straps to Bag

1. Slip a Strap end through a rectangle ring. Fold over 1½″, making sure the folded end is facing the bag, not the outside.

2. Edgestitch and topstitch the strap in place.

3. Thread the other Strap end through the rectangle slider, then slip it through the second rectangle ring, then through the slider again. Make sure that the center bar of the rectangle slider is facing the bag, not the outside. Fold over 1½″.

4. Edgestitch and topstitch the strap in place.

Accordion Card File Wallet

Finished size: 3˝ wide × 4˝ tall × ½˝ deep

This accordion-style card file uses hand-dyed kraft-tex, lining fabric, and hardware to make an impressive wallet. Interior Straps are there to hold folded bills.

Photo by Nissa Brehmer

About the Maker

Artist: Mary E. Flynn

Instagram: @maryelf

See Mary's artist bio (page 49).

Materials

kraft-tex Basics, Vintage, or Designer:* At least 8½″ × 11″

Foam stabilizer: Sew-in or fusible, 4″ × 9″ scrap

Bag lining fabric: 5″ × 9″ scrap (or use white fabric, to dye)

Kiss-lock purse frame: 3″ wide

Coordinating thread

Perle cotton #5 or #8

* Buying prewashed kraft-tex, or prewashing it yourself, is helpful for this project.

Tools and Supplies

Fabric paints: Such as Jacquard Dye-Na-Flow or Marabu Textil

Bone folder or pressing tool: Such as in Alex Anderson's 4-in-1 Essential Sewing Tool (by C&T Publishing)

Fabric clips: Such as Clover Wonder Clips, or binder clips

Ruler

Awl or stiletto: Such as in Alex Anderson's 4-in-1 Essential Sewing Tool (by C&T Publishing)

Crewel needle

Cutting

kraft-tex

• Cut 1 piece 3″ × 8½″ for Card File Exterior.

• Cut 1 piece 4½″ × 8½″ for Card File Side Pleats.

• Cut 2 pieces 3″ × 1½″ for Card File Interior Straps.

Lining fabric *or* white fabric

• Cut 1 piece 4¼″ × 8½″ for Card File Interior.

Foam

• Cut 1 piece 3″ × 8½″ for Card File Interior.

Make It

Color the kraft-tex

Follow the instructions in Rainbow Crossbody Bag, Color the kraft-tex (page 50). If dying white fabric for the lining, dye the white fabric in the same manner.

Prepare the Interior Foam Backing

1. Pin or clip the long sides of the fabric Card File Interior to the long sides of the foam Card File Interior, wrong sides together. Stitch. (The fabric will be wider and will bunch up in the middle.)

2. Turn right sides out. Press the seams.

INTERIOR STRAPS

1. Using a ruler, measure 1½˝ down from the top of the Card File interior. Place the Interior Strap alongside the ruler, line it up with the outside edges of the Card File interior, and clip it in place.

2. Repeat at the other end of the Card File interior with the second Interior Strap.

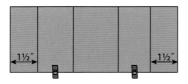

CARD FILE EXTERIOR

1. Measure 4˝ down from each short end, and score a line. Fold on the scored lines, making a bottom for the card file.

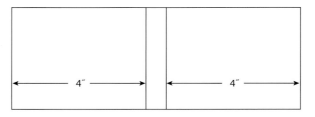

2. Clip this together with the card file interior, wrong sides together.

SIDE ACCORDION PLEATS

1. Use a ruler and bone folder to score the pleats, as shown (below). Score the first line ¾˝ away from a short end. Continue across the kraft-tex, scoring 15 lines, 1 line every ½˝. The last line should fall ¾˝ from the opposite short end.

2. Fold and press with a bone folder along all the score lines. Turn the kraft-tex over and fold the creases back on themselves.

3. Cut across the accordion pleats at the center, making 2 sets of side pleats, 2¼˝ × 8½˝.

4. Arrange the folds accordion style (mountain > valley > mountain > valley) across the entire piece, as shown.

¾˝	½˝	½˝	½˝	½˝	½˝	½˝	½˝	½˝	½˝	½˝	½˝	½˝	½˝	½˝	¾˝

Black is a mountain fold; red is a valley fold.

Card File Construction

All seam allowances are ¼˝.

ATTACH SIDE ACCORDION PLEATS TO CARD FILE

1. Use a ruler to measure 1˝ down from the top of the card file interior. Place a set of accordion pleats alongside the ruler, lined up with the outside edges of the card file interior, on the right in relation to the top of that side. Clip it in place over the interior strap. You'll have 8 folds facing the inside, while the longer ends and 7 folds will face the outside. Clip the ends of the pleats together near the center.

2. Edgestitch down the right side of the card file, catching the side of the pleat unit and the strap beneath it. Stop stitching with the needle down just at the center of the wallet.

3. Place the other edge of the pleat unit alongside the other end, 1˝ from the top edge. Continue to edgestitch through to the top of the card file, securing all pleats and the right side of the second interior strap.

4. Repeat Steps 1–3 for the left side of the card file.

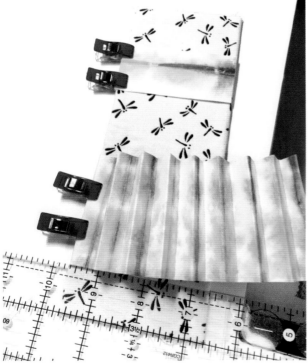

Instructional photos by Mary E. Flynn

ATTACH CARD FILE TO FRAME

1. Place the top edge of the card file into the purse frame as far as it will go. Use a fine-point pen to mark the holes on the card file.

2. Place the top of the card file on a surface that you can punch through with an awl or stiletto (such as a portable pressing board, piece of corrugated cardboard, or scrap of foam core). Use the awl or stiletto to poke holes through the kraft-tex at each marked point.

3. Repeat Steps 1 and 2 for the top of the other side of the card file.

4. Tuck one end of the card file back into the metal frame. Use an awl to smooth and tuck in the fabric on the interior. Hold the card file up to the light to be sure the punched holes line up with the holes in the frame.

5. Thread a crewel needle with a 12˝ length of perle cotton. Insert the needle into the top of the card file. Exit through the first hole of the kraft-tex and bring the thread through the first hole in the metal frame.

6. Pull the thread taut, re-align the sewing holes to the frame, and take the next stitch to the frame.

7. Clip the card file to the frame hinge. Continue stitching across the frame through the card file.

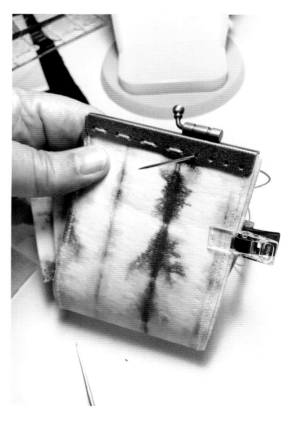

Instructional photos by Mary E. Flynn

8. Once you have stitched all the way across, turn around and stitch your way back to the beginning.

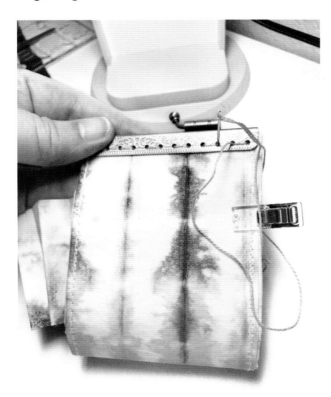

9. After the stitching is complete, take a final backstitch, doubling over your first stitch. From the inside, make a knot in the stitches. Push the needle out through the side of the card file, between the card file interior and exterior. Trim the thread close to the edge of the card file.

10. Repeat Steps 4–9 for the other side of the card file.

The flower embroidery design is a built-in design from the Janome 500e embroidery machine and is used by permission of Janome Canada. All other designs or photos belong to Linda Seemann-Korte.

Funky Zipper Pouches

Finished size: 9¾″ wide × 6″ tall × 3½″ deep

Try your hand at a zipper pouch that opens wide—or make many pouches! Using a different surface design treatment for each (machine embroidery, appliqué, paint sticks, or photo printing), you can make fun and fresh zippy bags that are as unique as you!

Photo by Blaine Korte

About the Maker

Artist: Linda Seemann-Korte

Instagram: @seemannkorte

Linda's sewing gene was inherited from her mother and grandmothers, who were all amazing seamstresses. In her sewing circles, Linda is known as an embellisher of jackets and a bag lady extraordinaire. For Linda, embellishment is the name of the game! She believes a pattern is just a guide—letting your creative juices flow and adding pockets and bling will make any creation stand out and be all your own!

Materials

kraft-tex Basics, Vintage, or Designer*

For inkjet-printed bag: 2 sheets 8½″ × 11″ and 1½″ × 3″ for tabs

For all other bags: 11″ × 18½″

* Buying prewashed kraft-tex, or prewashing it yourself, is helpful for this project.

Other Materials

Double-sided fusible web: ¼″ wide
(such as Steam-A-Seam 2, by The Warm Company)

Thread: To match or contrast

Fabric marker, disappearing pen, or chalk marker

Specific sewing machine feet (*optional*): Walking foot, open-toe foot, and/or zipper foot

Zipper tape and pull: 24″ long
(You will use only one side of zipper tape.)

OPTION 1: APPLIQUÉ

Appliqué template (*optional*)

Open-toe foot (*optional*)

OPTION 2: SHIVA PAINTSTIKS

Shiva Paintstik Oils

Stiff stencil brush

Paper towel

OPTION 3: MACHINE EMBROIDERY

Double-sided fusible web: 8½″ × 11″
(such as Steam-A-Seam 2)

Embroidery thread

Embroidery hoop and machine

Tear-away stabilizer

Washi tape

OPTION 4: INKJET PRINTING

Image to print

Inkjet printer

Cutting

kraft-tex for inkjet-printed bag

• Cut 2 pieces 8½˝ × 11˝ for bag.

• Cut 2 pieces 1½˝ × 1½˝ for tabs.

kraft-tex for other bags

• Cut 1 piece of kraft-tex 11˝ × 17˝ for bag.

• Cut 2 pieces 1½˝ × 1½˝ for tabs.

Embellish It

Option 1: Appliqué

1. Design the appliqué, trace it on kraft-tex, and cut it out.

2. Apply a couple strips of double-sided fusible web on the back, and iron it on to the front of the bag.

3. Stitch around the perimeter, using an open-toe foot to see where you are going!

Option 2: Shiva Paintstiks

Shiva Paintstiks are oil-based paints. They get a skin on them after use, which needs to be shaved off with a craft knife prior to use.

1. Apply the paint from the first color stick directly onto the kraft-tex, and use a stiff round stencil brush to spread it and blend it. Continue in this manner with other colors, using a new brush for each color to ensure that the color is vibrant.

2. Once you are finished designing, let the paint sit for 24 hours.

3. Press with an iron to heat set it, being sure to cover the ironing surface and the top of the kraft-tex, so the paint does not end up on the iron or surface.

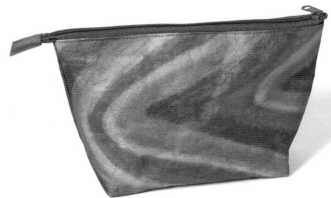

Option 3: Machine Embroidery

When machine embroidering, kraft-tex needs to be stabilized with fabric on the back. kraft-tex will get holes if it is stitched more than twice in one spot!

1. Cut a piece of double-sided fusible web the same size as 1 bag piece, and iron it onto the kraft-tex. When cool, peel off the paper and iron a piece of fabric on the top.

tips

You can use strips of double-sided fusible web if you don't have a piece of it large enough. You just need to make sure the fabric will be under the embroidery.

A batik or hand-dyed fabric with a high thread count is less likely to fray.

2. Hoop one layer of tear-away stabilizer in your embroidery hoop. Float the kraft-tex over the embroidery hoop. Use paper tape (such as washi) to tape the kraft-tex in place on top of the stabilizer, centering it where you wish to have the embroidery. Embroider as desired.

Option 4: Inkjet Printing

Choose a photo that you wish to have printed on kraft-tex. Insert an 8½″ × 11″ sheet of kraft-tex into the printer. Print and repeat for the other sheet (second side of the bag).

Make It

All seams are ¼˝.

1. Place the 2 bag pieces right side together, and sew only one side seam. The seams need to be back stitched.

2. Press the seam to one side.

3. Cut a length of zipper tape 24˝ long. Separate the zipper, you will only be using one side of the zipper tape. Set the pull aside.

4. With the kraft-tex right side up, lay the zipper tape along the longest edge of the bag, with the wrong side of the zipper up and the teeth down toward the bottom of the bag. Make sure that the edge of the zipper tape is ¼˝ down from the edge of the bag, and the zipper extends 1˝ past the edge of the kraft-tex on each end. Use clips to hold the zipper in place.

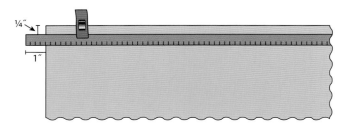

5. Use a fabric marker to mark the zipper tape with a line ½˝ in from each edge. This is where you will start and stop sewing the zipper.

6. Put the needle down ½˝ from the mark to begin sewing the zipper. Sew backward until you reach the mark, then go forward. When you get to the other mark, back up for ½˝ to secure the seam.

7. Press the zipper seam.

8. Sew the other side seam, making sure the zipper tape is out of the way. Unfold the zipper edge so you can sew right across the entire seam. Press both side seams to the front of the bag.

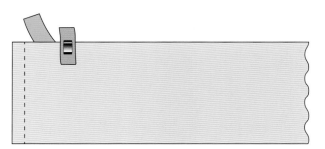

9. If you are using 2 pieces of the kraft-tex, sew the bottom of the bag now. Make sure both side seams are folded to the same side before you stitch the bottom.

If you are using 1 piece of kraft-tex, mark the center of the bag so you will know where to place side seams when you box the corners.

10. Box the corners of the bag to create a bottom. At one bottom corner, match the side seam of the bag to the bottom seam or center of the bag, and crease the kraft-tex to form a triangle. The seam allowance at the bottom of the bag folds the opposite way to the side seams to reduce bulk and give a neat finish.

11. Using a quilting ruler, line up the 45° mark with one edge of the triangle, and the straight edge 1½˝ from the point of the triangle. Draw a 3˝ straight line across the triangle for your sewing line.

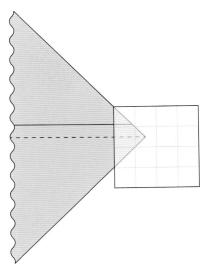

Box the bag corners.

12. Sew along this line. You may wish to sew a second line ⅛˝ to the right of the first sewing line to make a stronger bottom. Trim the seam ¼˝ past the stitching line.

13. Repeat Steps 10–12 for the other corner.

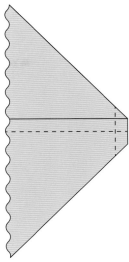

Trim ¼˝ past stitching line.

14. Carefully turn the bag right side out. Take your time, it takes a bit of fiddling!

15. Increase your stitch length, and topstitch the top edge of the bag. Stitch all the way around the bag just below the zipper on the kraft-tex.

16. Attach the zipper pull, threading one end of the zipper tape a short way into the pull, and then the other.

17. Iron 2 strips of ¼˝ double-sided fusible web onto each zipper tab. Let cool and remove the paper. Place a tab over each side of the zipper tape, and iron in place. Stitch around all 4 sides about ⅛˝ from the edge to stitch the tab to the zipper tape. Do this twice. Trim the tab after it is sewn.

Mini Suitcase

Finished size: 6″ wide × 4″ tall × 1⅝″ deep

Travel in style, even if it's just to your desk, with this petite piece of luggage made from kraft-tex! The perfect storage spot for odds and ends, like sewing clips and secret notes, the Mini Suitcase also makes a great gift. The wax treatment can really change the look and feel of kraft-tex.

About the Maker

Artist: Susan Leath

Susan is a desert-dweller living in Southwest Arizona. She is happiest and in her zone when sitting in front of a sewing machine. She loves to experiment with different methods to shape, color, and texture kraft-tex to create handmade items. It just takes an idea and the determination to make something new. For Susan, when using inks, fabric, glue, or a sewing machine, there really is no limit as to what one can create!

Materials

kraft-tex Basics or Vintage—Natural:* 4 sheets 8½″ × 11″ or equivalent

Lightweight quilting fabric: 8″ × 15″ for lining (or use decorative paper)

White glue

Iron-on transfer paper: For light fabric, 1 sheet 8½″ × 11″ (or use printed fabric)

Wax: 50/50 paraffin/beeswax mixture

Thin wire: Or use paper clips

Card stock: 2 sheets 8½″ × 11″

Bobbin: To trace corner protectors

Parchment (silicone) paper

Brown paper: Such as from a paper grocery bag

Needle-nose pliers

Tweezers

Binder clips: ½″ wide

* Buying prewashed kraft-tex, or prewashing it yourself, is helpful for this project.

Cutting

From the Mini Suitcase patterns (page 107 and pullout page P1), prepare templates for the lid, bottom, handle A, handle B, strap A, strap B, cardboard bottom, and cardboard lid.

kraft-tex

- Cut 1 from lid.
- Cut 1 from bottom.
- Cut 1 from handle A.
- Cut 2 from handle B.
- Cut 2 from strap A.
- Cut 2 from strap B.
- Cut 1 hinge 1½″ × 6¼″.

Card stock

- Cut 1 cardboard bottom.
- Cut 1 cardboard lid.

Lightweight quilting fabric or decorative paper

Reduce/trim the outline/size of the lining by a hair to fit inside the card stock suitcase base.

- Cut 1 cardboard bottom.
- Cut 1 cardboard lid.

Make It

Apply Wax Coating to kraft-tex

1. Scrunch dry kraft-tex to get a wrinkled, leather-like texture.

2. Melt the 50/50 paraffin/beeswax mixture, using a candle warmer in a glass or aluminum container *or* a double-boiler.

3. Brush melted wax covering over one side of the kraft-tex.

4. Sandwich the kraft-tex between 2 pieces of parchment paper. Apply a hot iron, allowing the wax to melt into the kraft-tex.

5. Sandwich the kraft-tex between 2 pieces of brown paper. Apply a hot iron to flatten, and to absorb heavy wax areas.

Assemble the Card Stock Base

1. Assemble the cardboard bottom and lid pieces, scoring and folding where indicated on the pattern with dashed lines. Using white glue, glue the 4 end tabs to the *inside* to form each box corner. I recommend using needle-nose pliers or tweezers to get good glue adhesion to the corners/edges.

2. Cover the card stock bottom with the kraft-tex bottom piece. Align the box edges with the kraft-tex dashed lines that indicate fold lines. *Be sure not to prefold or score the kraft-tex fold lines; instead, fold each side and apply white glue to the box sides as you go.* Use binder clips to hold the sides in place while the glue dries.

3. Use the same process to cover the card stock lid with the kraft-tex lid piece.

Make the Suitcase and Lid Lining

1. Fold down all sides of the cut linings. Apply white glue to the bottom of the mini suitcase lining, and glue the bottom of the lining down first, then the 4 sides.

2. Glue the bottom portion of the lid lining. Then, glue *only* 3 sides of the lining, leaving the back unglued.

3. Test fit the hinge piece and trim as needed to fit inside the lid. Glue the hinge to the inside back of the lid, then glue the lining on top of the hinge.

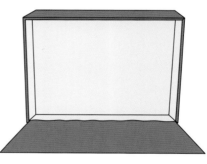

4. Apply a heavy line of glue on the back, where the hinge meets the lid.

5. Place the lid on the bottom and glue the hinge to the back of the bottom. Let the glue dry overnight.

Make the Corner Protectors

1. Using the side of a bobbin as a circle template for the corner protectors, cut 8 circles from kraft-tex. Use a marking tool to divide each protector into 4 sections, then cut out a quarter-section from each.

2. Fold 2 sides as shown, and glue to the corner of the suitcase. Repeat for all 8 corners.

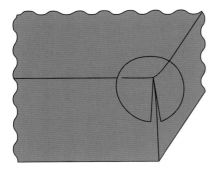

Make the Handle

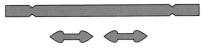

MAKE THE HANDLE HARDWARE

1. Grasp handle A with the needle-nosed pliers and mark the pliers where the width matches the handle A.

2. Wrap wire around the pliers at the marked line to shape the hardware used to assemble the handle. I straightened a small paper clip to make the ones shown. Make 4 pieces; you will use 2 as buckles for the straps later.

3. Shape the kraft-tex handle A to add a curve. (*Optional:* Glue an additional smaller piece of kraft-tex to the inside to give it more weight.)

4. Fold up the ends where the notches were cut, and slip on one of the metal hardware pieces over it, as shown. Glue together all pieces to form the completed handle.

5. Fold and glue the handle B pieces to each end. Use tweezers and a binder clip to hold the glued pieces in place until they dry, as shown.

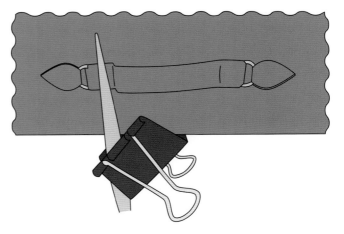

Note

When gluing the complete handle on the suitcase base, keep in mind where the lid will be when closed.

Make the Straps and Buckles

1. Cut 2 buckle pins ¾″ long from a thin wire or paper clip.

2. Place a pin on each strap A. Glue the buckle pin ¼″ beyond the slit, as shown.

3. Fold down the end flaps of strap A and glue over a buckle. The pin should lie in the gap in the buckle. Hold it in place with tweezers until the glue has set. Trim the pin even with the buckle.

Close-up of buckle assembly

4. Following the template, poke pin holes in the ends of the straps B to serve as buckle holes.

5. Glue each strap A on top of the suitcase, and each strap B on the bottom of the suitcase, each placed ⅞″ from the side, as shown in the project photo (at right).

Snappy Slim Wallet

Finished size: 3˝ wide × 4⅜˝ tall

Pick up a measuring tape from your local discount store—it's one of the magic materials to make this wallet "snap"! With a slim profile and the image transfer of your choice, this kraft-tex wallet really looks and wears like leather.

About the Maker

Artist: Susan Leath

See Susan's artist bio (page 75).

Materials

kraft-tex Basics or Vintage—Natural or White:* 4″ × 5″

Solid quilting fabric: ¼ yard

Fleece iron-on interfacing: 5″ × 6″

Metal measuring tape:** ½″–⅝″ wide × 5″,
to be cut and used in wallet construction

White glue

White screen-printing ink for paper (*optional*):
Not needed if using white kraft-tex

Iron-on transfer paper: For light fabric, 8½″ × 11″

Wax: 50/50 paraffin/beeswax mixture

Parchment (silicone) paper

Brown paper: Such as from a paper grocery bag

** Buying prewashed kraft-tex, or prewashing it yourself,
is helpful for this project.*

*** You can find a metal measuring tape at your local dollar
or discount store.*

Cutting

*From Snappy Slim Wallet patterns A–E (pages 109
and 110), prepare templates.*

kraft-tex

- Cut 1 piece A.

Quilting fabric

- Cut 3 piece B.

- Cut 1 piece C, do not cut out oval.

- Cut 1 piece D, do not cut out oval.

Fleece Interfacing

- Cut 2 pieces E.

Snap closure

- Cut 2 pieces 2⅜″ from a ½″–⅝″-wide metal tape
  measure. Use a pair of nonsewing scissors to
  round the end corners, and cover the ends in a
  small piece of electrical tape so the metal doesn't
  poke through the fabric.

Make It

1. Scrunch kraft-tex to create a leather-like texture. Hand smooth it to flatten it a bit.

2. Using screen-printing ink, apply an even coat onto one side of the kraft-tex. Allow to dry overnight. Once the ink is dry, cover with parchment paper and apply a hot iron to set the ink. Set aside.

3. Prepare your image on the iron-on transfer paper, following the manufacturer's instructions. Transfer the image, then trace and cut the kraft-tex piece.

4. Iron the transfer onto the white painted area of the kraft-tex piece, then apply an even, thin coat of the melted-wax mixture (see Mini Suitcase, Apply Wax Coating to kraft-tex, Step 2, page 76) over the entire image. Place the kraft-tex piece between 2 pieces of parchment paper and apply a hot iron to melt the wax into the kraft-tex. Absorb thick wax areas by placing the kraft-tex between 2 pieces of brown paper to ensure an even coat of wax.

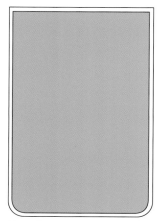

Transfer image onto kraft-tex.

5. Fuse the interfacing E to the wrong side of one fabric B piece.

6. Place kraft-tex piece A and the piece B from Step 5, *right sides together*, and sew across the top edge, using a ¼″ seam allowance. Fold over, *wrong sides now together*, and press the top seam. Topstitch ⅛″ from the top edge.

7. Below the ⅛″ top seam on piece A/B, place the metal snap-closure strip and mark a line to hold the strip in place, allowing enough room to slide it in later. Remove the snap-closure and sew on the line.

8. Repeat Steps 5–7, this time using 2 fabric B pieces.

9. Fold pieces C and D at fold lines and lightly crease. Apply a layer of white glue in the fold crease and corners, then fold the fabric piece in half, lining up all edges. Smooth down flat. Set aside to let the glue dry. Once dry, cut out the gray "thumb" curves.

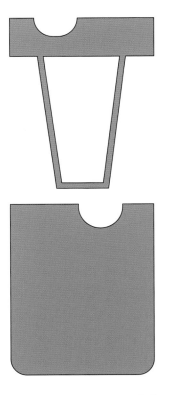

10. Topstitch the card slots ⅛″ from top edge. It isn't necessary to topstitch the curve at

the thumb area, since it has been glued together.

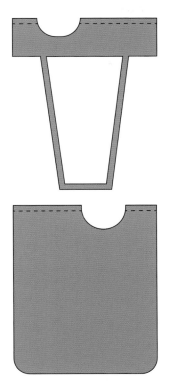

11. Place piece D on top of piece B/B with the top edge ¼″ below the top edge of piece B/B. Stitch together ¼″ from the lower edge of piece D.

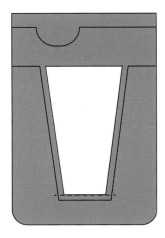

12. Sandwich all pieces together in this order, from bottom to top:

- Printed wallet front (piece A/B), face down
- Wallet back (piece B/B)
- Taller pocket (piece D)
- Shorter pocket (piece C)

Use clips to hold the pieces in place while sewing.

13. Starting at top right corner, with a 3.5-wide zigzag edge stitch, sew the edges closed. Stop on second side 1¼″ from the top. Insert the snap-closure metal strips with the curves facing in. Continue sewing the zigzag edge seam to the top.

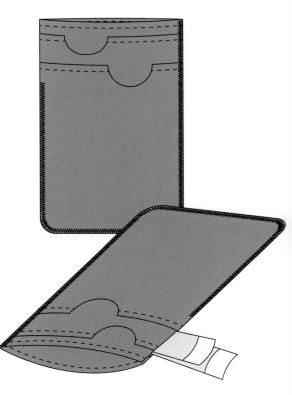

Tuck Flap Wallet

Finished size: 4⅜″ wide × 3″ tall

With two pockets for your ID and credit cards, this skinny wallet will become an instant favorite. Experiment with a paraffin wax mixture to give the kraft-tex an instant sheen, and use an image-transfer technique to personalize your card keeper.

About the Maker

Artist: Susan Leath

See Susan's artist bio (page 75).

Materials

kraft-tex Basics or Vintage—Natural: 8½″ × 11″

Muslin quilting fabric: Unbleached, lightweight, solid color, 8½″ × 11″

White glue

Screen-printing ink for paper (*optional*): Use if you wish to change the color of the kraft-tex.

Iron-on transfer paper: For light fabric, 8½″ × 11″

Wax: 50/50 paraffin/beeswax mixture

Parchment (silicone) paper

Brown paper: Such as from a paper grocery bag

Cutting

From the Tuck Flap Wallet patterns (pages 108 and 109), prepare templates A–C.

kraft-tex

- Cut 1 piece A.
- Cut 1 piece B.
- Cut 2 piece C.

Fabric

- Cut 1 piece A.
- Cut 1 piece B.
- Cut 1 piece C.

Make It

1. Scrunch kraft-tex to create a leather-like texture. Hand smooth it to flatten it a bit.

2. Using screen-printing ink, apply an even coat onto one side of the kraft-tex. Allow to dry overnight. Once the ink is dry, cover with parchment paper and apply a hot iron to set the ink.

3. Apply an even, thin coat of the melted-wax mixture (see Mini Suitcase, Apply Wax Coating to kraft-tex, page 76) over the painted side of the kraft-tex. Place the kraft-tex piece

between 2 pieces of parchment paper and apply a hot iron to melt the wax into the kraft-tex. Absorb thick wax areas by placing the kraft-tex piece between 2 pieces of brown paper.

4. If desired, use a permanent marker matching the screen-printing ink to color the cut edges of kraft-tex.

5. Prepare your image on the iron-on transfer image, following the manufacturer's instructions. Transfer the image.

6. Glue the fabric image to the unpainted side of the kraft-tex. Trim the image fabric following the shape of the kraft-tex piece, using the template's shaded area. Using 1 piece of fabric cut from piece B, glue the fabric to the bottom of piece A.

Glue the fabric image and fabric B onto kraft-tex A.

7. Glue the fabric piece B to the wrong side of the kraft-tex piece B. Do the same with the fabric piece C and a kraft-tex piece C. The other kraft-tex piece C does not need fabric backing; it will be used as the reinforcing strip in the fold of the wallet.

8. Sew piece C without fabric on the back across the lower "fold" of the wallet.

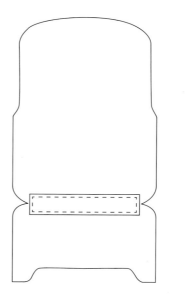

9. Using a zigzag stitch, edgestitch the long sides of the fabric-lined piece C, the top edge of piece B, and all edges of piece A.

10. Fold the bottom of the wallet up, placing piece B behind the folded-up portion of piece A. Place the fabric-lined piece C across the inside of the wallet, using clips to temporarily hold it in place. Zigzag stitch along the left and right sides to secure.

Cut Mesh Bag

Finished size: 15˝ wide × 13½˝ tall × 7˝ deep

Experiment with cutting kraft-tex in a way that makes it expand into a totally new material: cut mesh! This lightweight bag looks three-dimensional, but it's made from a flat piece of kraft-tex. Inside is a fabric drawstring sack for small items—perfect for shopping or going out for coffee with friends!

Photo by T. McColl

About the Maker

Artist: Lightning McStitch

Website:

bartacksandsingletrack.com

By day, she goes by the name of Shelley. A veterinarian, cyclist, gym junkie, and mum to two kids, she loves to sew at night-time, when the house is quiet. She challenges herself to make all the clothes for herself and her kids. She loves how crafting offers the freedom to fail, yet is so satisfying when successful. For Lightning, you never know what you can or can't do until you try!

Materials

kraft-tex Basics or Vintage—Chocolate: 18″ × 25″

Calico, cotton, or linen fabric: 40″ wide, ½ yard for internal sack

Cording or cotton rope: 35″ long for drawstring

Thread:

- *Sewing:* To match fabric sack

- *Topstitching or upholstery-weight:* To match kraft-tex

* Buying prewashed kraft-tex, or prewashing it yourself, is helpful for this project.

Tools

Glue stick, washi tape, or removable adhesive tape

Tracing or parchment paper

Tracing wheel: Or spatula knife or other pointed object to transfer pattern markings to kraft-tex

Bodkin or safety pin

Cutting

From the Cut Mesh Bag patterns (page 112 and pullout page P1), prepare the base, handle, and drawcord tab templates.

kraft-tex

- Cut 1 piece 18″ × 18″ for bag.

- From the remaining 18″ × 7″ piece, cut:

  2 from Base template

  4 from Handle template

  2 from Drawcord Tab template

Fabric

- Cut 1 from Base template with the seam allowance (dashed line) added in.

- Cut 1 piece 14″ × 25½″ for main bag piece.

- Cut 1 piece 1½″ × 25½″ for drawstring casing.

Make the Cut Mesh Bag

Create a Cutting Template

Using a nonsmudge pen, trace the solid lines of the cutting pattern (pullout page P1) onto tracing or parchment paper to make a cutting template. To help align the tracing, also trace the horizontal and vertical center lines.

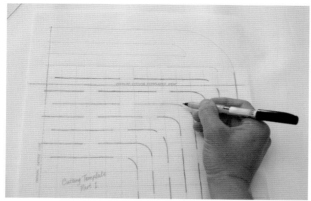

Instructional photos by Lightning McStitch

Cut the kraft-tex

1. Using a pencil softly, draw 1 line bisecting the square horizontally and 1 bisecting vertically. The lines will cross at the center point of the square.

2. Position the cutting template tracing in the top right quadrant of the kraft-tex square. Ensure that the outer edge lines meet the edge of the kraft-tex and the traced center lines are aligned with the center lines drawn on the kraft-tex. Use removable adhesive tape to hold the traced template in place.

3. Using the tracing wheel (or other pointed object), trace over all the template lines, pushing firmly to mark the kraft-tex. You don't need to go over the center lines.

4. Flip the traced template facedown and position it in the top left quadrant. Align the center lines and outer edge lines, and continue to trace and mark as before. Repeat this process to transfer the template markings to all 4 corners.

5. Cut over the traced lines with a sharp knife.

6. Apply glue to a base piece and glue it over the center of the main square. The base piece should fit just inside the first ring of mesh cuts. Glue the second base to the other side in the same way, aligning them with each other as precisely as possible.

7. Glue the handle pieces to the handle sections of the main square. Use the penciled center line to help position the handle in the middle. In the same manner as the base, glue another handle on the reverse side, aligning them precisely. Repeat for the other handle with the remaining 2 handle pieces.

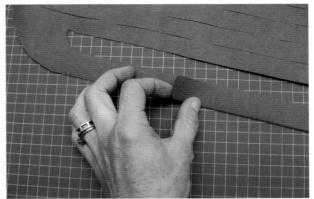

8. Stitch through all 3 layers of kraft-tex about ⅛˝ from the edge to secure the bag base and handle pieces. The upper, more visible, sides of the handles will be on the same side as the outer, more visible, side of the base.

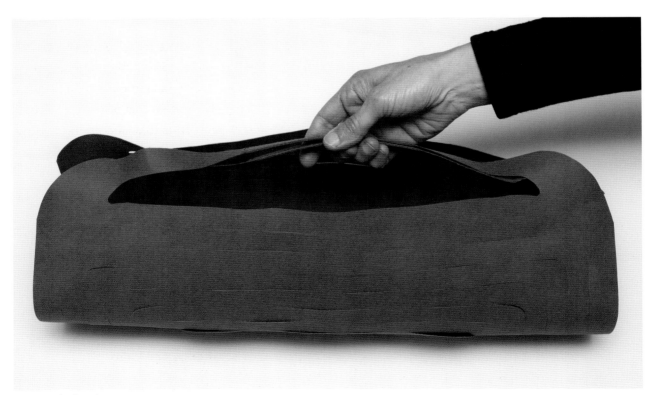

Bag ready for shaping

Shaping the Bag

1. Immerse the completed bag in warm water. Shake off the excess water.

2. Pull the sides and corners away from the base to open up the mesh. Bring the short sides together, then the front and back with the handles together. Stretch and pull the mesh inward and upward until you like the shape.

3. Find a heavy object about the same size as the bag's base, like a heavy book or a baking dish. With the weight on the base, hang the bag to dry.

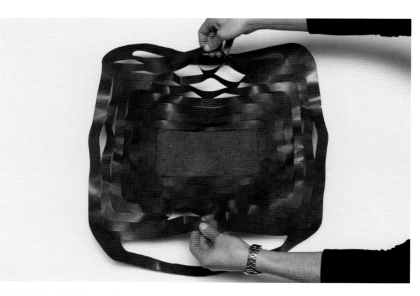

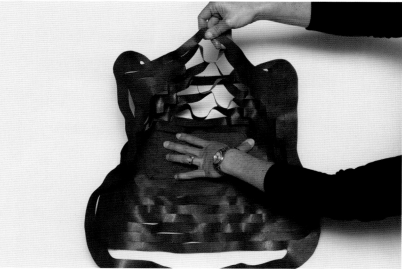

Instructional photos by Lightning McStitch

Make the Fabric Sack

1. Mark the center points (notches) on the long and short sides of the base fabric piece.

2. With the wrong side up, press each long edge of the drawstring casing to the center. At each short end, open out the pressed folds and turn the ends in by ⅝˝. Refold the original creases and press well.

3. On the main bag piece, mark a horizontal line 4˝ from the top of the rectangle. Pin the casing, right side up, to the right side of the main bag piece, positioning the casing over this marked line. The casing should be ⅝˝ shorter than the bag at each end.

4. Edgestitch each long side of the casing, leaving the short sides open.

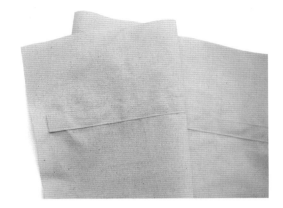

5. Pin the short ends of the main bag piece right sides together. Stitch with a ½˝ seam, making sure not to catch the open ends of the casing in your seam. Finish the seam allowances and press to one side.

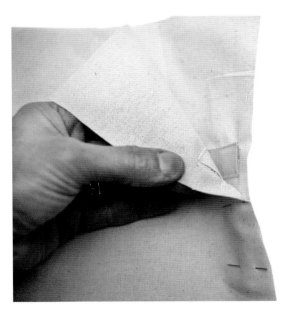

6. Mark the lower edge of the bag opposite the stitched seam, dividing the bag in half. Bring this marked line up to the stitched seam, and fold the bag again to find and mark the quarter points.

7. Pin the bag to the base, right sides together: Align the bag seam with one of the halfway marks on a long side of the base. Pin the 3 other quarter point marks. Pin toward each corner. Use plenty of pins to fit the bag to the corners of the base.

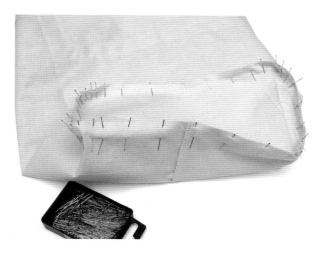

8. Stitch the bag to the base with a ½″ seam. Finish the seam allowances together with a zigzag stitch.

9. Hem the top of the bag: Fold the raw edge ¼″ to the wrong side. Press again to the wrong side by 1″. Edgestitch the first fold to finish the hem.

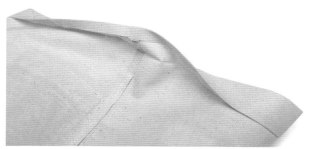

Instructional photos by Lightning McStitch

10. Using a bodkin or safety pin, thread the drawstring through the casing.

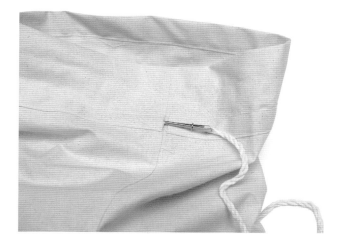

11. Fold each kraft-tex drawstring tab along the central fold line. With the drawstring cord entering the tab at the open, short end, stitch around the tab to secure it.

Print and Stitch Purse

Finished size: 11¾″ wide × 9½″ tall × 4″ deep

Create an original purse with a design you print yourself! Using a simple, repeated shape—like a rectangle, triangle, or square—and adding embroidery gives the overall design more texture and interest. Match the purse handle colors to the color of the ink, or switch it up for your personal style.

Photo by David Bamattre

About the Maker

Artist: Colette Moscrop

Website: colettemoscrop.com

Colette is a printer, a textile and product designer, and a workshop tutor. A passion for rich colors, simple patterns, and the urban lifestyle of London feed into her sketchbook, resulting in modern, hand screen–printed textiles with a hand-drawn quality. Making items to be used and loved for many years are at the heart of Colette's ethos; she believes the process of creating something meaningful and true to oneself is a luxury worth savoring. Outside of the studio, Colette explores London with her daughters and husband, trawls vintage fairs for 1940's dresses, and drinks tea.

Materials

kraft-tex Basics, Vintage, or Designer: * 1 yard

Cotton fabric: 1 fat quarter 18″ × 22″ for lining

Purse handles: 1 pair, plastic, U-shaped, approximately 6¾″ × 4¾″

Textile screen-printing ink: Such as Permaset Aqua or Speedball

Embroidery or perle cotton thread

Sponge

Potato: Medium to large for printing

Sharp knife: To cut the potato

Small old plate: For ink

Fabric pencil

Newsprint: To protect work surface

* Buying prewashed kraft-tex, or prewashing it yourself, is helpful for this project.

Cutting

From the Print and Stitch Purse pattern (pullout page P1), prepare a purse body/lining template.

kraft-tex

• Cut 2 from purse body/lining.*

• Cut 2 pieces 15″ × 3″ for facing.

• Cut 4 pieces 3″ × ½″ for tabs for handle.

Lining

• Cut 2 purse body/lining, following the directions on the pattern.*

* On the wrong side of both pieces, mark the dart positions and the center of the top of the purse.

Printing the Design

1. Cut a potato in half, and carve the design you want to print into the center of the potato. Cut down about ½″ into the potato, and cut away any excess, leaving the carved design protruding. Wash and dry the potato with a kitchen towel.

tip

Lay down old fabric or newspaper to protect your work surface.

2. Spoon a small amount of ink onto an old plate. Using the sponge, dab the ink to cover an area of the sponge evenly. Dab the ink evenly onto the carved design on the potato.

tip

Try practicing on some brown paper or calico to map out your design and get a feel for printing. When you're more confident, practice on a scrap of kraft-tex before printing directly onto the project kraft-tex.

Print a test run.

3. Applying even pressure and making sure your potato doesn't slip, press the potato, ink side down, where you would like it on the right side of the kraft-tex purse body. Aim to fill less than half the bag front—the unprinted space allows your design to breathe. Continue printing until you are happy with the design.

4. Let the ink dry, then heat set on the reverse side, following the ink manufacturer's instructions. This is usually done with a hot iron.

tip

You'll get imperfect shapes and misprints. Don't be tempted to go over them! Leave them and embrace the difference that hand printing creates.

Instructional photos by Colette Moscrop

Hand-Stitched Details

1. Using a denim needle in your sewing machine, and removing the thread, "sew" and create holes where you would like your hand stitching to go. Set the stitch length to 4 for most of the lines; to add a little variety, change the stitch length on a few lines. To add some interest and keep the eye moving, stagger the lines and vary their length.

2. With decorative embroidery thread or cotton perle, stitch a simple running stitch in the holes you created. If you need to add an additional hole at the end of a row, pierce with your needle or a thumbtack.

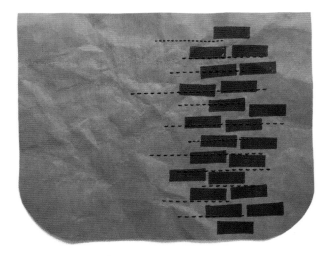

tip

Choose an embroidery thread that won't overpower your printing, but will complement it.

Sew the Purse

Backtack all seams.

1. Thread a small kraft-tex tab for the handles through the hole in the handle. Fold the tab and stitch the ends together, about ⅛″ from the edge. Repeat with the second tab.

2. Measure the gap between the tabs and mark the position of the handles on the top edge of the purse. Use the center mark you made earlier to help center the handles.

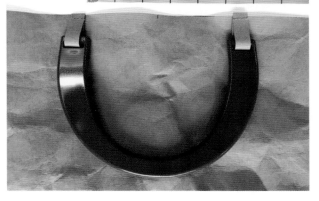

3. Stitch the handle tabs to the main body of the purse, using a ¼″ seam allowance. Repeat on the other purse piece. When looking at the purse piece right side up, the handle should be attached and appear upside down in a U-shape.

4. Sew the darts in the kraft-tex. On one purse body, finger-press the darts up, and on the other purse body, finger-press the darts down. This reduces the bulk.

5. Use sewing clips to hold the front and back pieces together. Machine sew an accurate ½˝ seam allowance around the sides and base of the purse.

Instructional photos by Colette Moscrop

6. Clip the curved corners. Stagger the cuts on the front and back to create a smoother curve. Keep the purse inside out.

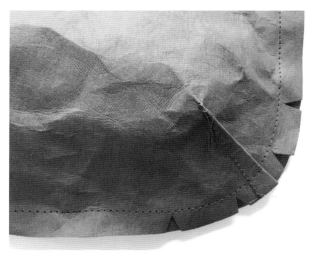

7. Using an accurate ½˝ seam allowance, sew together a facing to a purse body/lining to make a front lining. Press the seam toward the lining. Repeat to make a back lining. Sew the front lining to the back lining, leaving a 4˝ gap between the darts at the base. Turn the lining right side out.

8. Ensure that the facing and the body of your purse are exactly the same in circumference at the top of the purse. Place the facing with lining inside the purse, right sides together, and join along the top with sewing clips.

9. With the body of the purse facing the feed dogs, and the facing on top, sew *slowly* all the way around the top of the purse with a ½″ seam allowance.

10. Gently push the purse right side out through the 4″ hole in the lining. Use your fingers to gently ease out the curves, and wiggle the seams a little to get them fully turned through.

11. Finger-press the top edge of the purse for a nice, crisp finish. Stitch the opening in the lining closed.

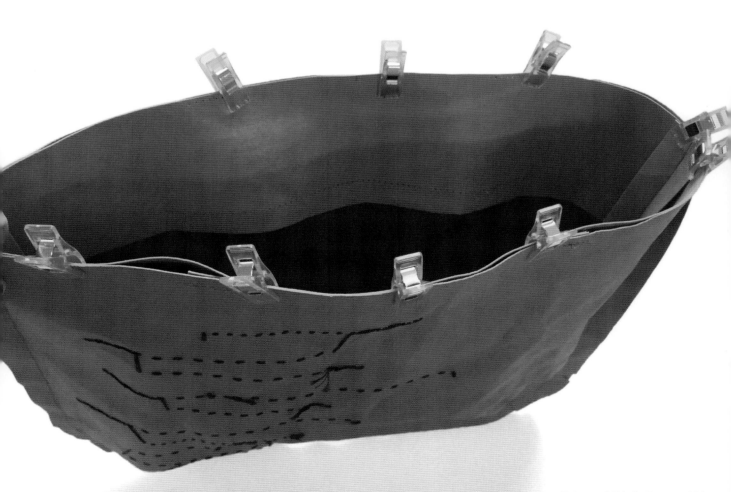

Baby Shoes

Finished size: 4⅜″ long × 2¼″ wide

Adorable and practical, these newborn to 12-month-size baby shoes make a great gift for new parents. kraft-tex details provide extra support for little toes. For older babies who crawl or walk, simply enlarge the pattern and add a nonslip sole instead of quilting cotton.

Photo by Mikki Collins

About the Maker

Artist: Vera Therrell

Website: etsy.com/shop/lausbub

Vera is the creator and owner of Lausbub, a small business for hand-sewn children's clothes and accessories. As a wife, military spouse, and mother to her wonderful little boy, she found a way to work from home doing what she loves. The brand name, *Lausbub*, originated from her German roots and translates to "rascal." Every single one of her pieces is made with passion and great attention to detail. She lives in Crestview, Florida.

Materials

kraft-tex Basics or Vintage—Natural:* 4″ × 8″

Main fabric: 100% cotton print, ¼ yard

Lining fabric: 100% cotton coordinating solid, ¼ yard

Elastic: ¼″ wide, ¼ yard
(You need only ⅓ yard for 9–12 month size.)

Coordinating thread

* Buying prewashed kraft-tex, or prewashing it yourself, is helpful for this project.

Cutting

Prewash all fabric and kraft-tex before cutting.

From the Baby Shoes patterns (pages 111 and 112), reduce or enlarge the patterns as noted below. Then prepare sole, toe, heel, toe accent A and B, and tab templates.

For 0–3 month size, reduce all patterns 86%.

For 6–9 month size, enlarge all patterns 106%.

For 9–12 month size, enlarge all patterns 120%.

kraft-tex

• Cut 1 toe accent A, and 1 toe accent A reversed.

• Cut 1 toe accent B, and 1 toe accent B reversed.

• Cut 2 tabs.

Main fabric

• Cut 2 sole pieces.

• Cut 2 toe pieces.

• Cut 2 heel pieces.

Lining

• Cut 2 sole pieces.

• Cut 2 toe pieces.

• Cut 2 heel pieces.

Make It

All seam allowances are ¼˝. Use small stitches.

1. Fold the heel tab in half and position the short raw edges in the middle of the lining heel piece. Put the main fabric heel piece on top, with the right sides facing. Sew the main fabric and lining along the top edge, and turn.

2. Topstitch ½˝ from the top edge to create the casing.

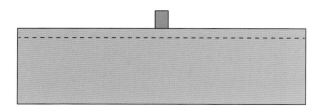

3. Cut 2 pieces of elastic 4⅛˝ long. Thread one piece through the casing, using a safety pin to guide it through. Sew a small stitch to tack the elastic at both ends of the casing.

4. Sew the kraft-tex accents on one main fabric toe, overlapping by ⅛˝.

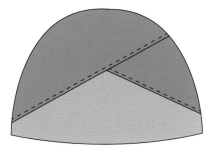

5. Line up the bottom corners of the main fabric heel with the corners of the main fabric toe, right sides facing. Stitch each side to secure.

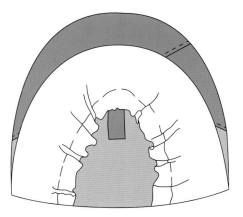

6. Match the lining toe on the opposite side, and stitch.

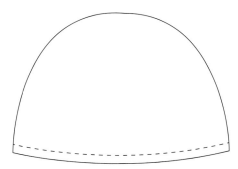

7. Turn right side out, and top-stitch ¼″ from the seam.

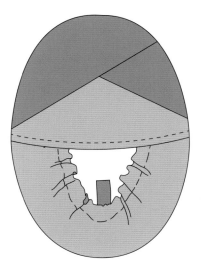

8. Match the triangle points of the outer sole and top shoe piece with right sides facing and pin together. Stitch all the way around.

9. Pin and sew the sole lining on the opposite side, leaving a 2″ opening in the back of the shoe.

10. Turn shoe through the 2″ hole. Sew the hole in the lining closed.

11. Turn shoe right side out.

12. Repeat Steps 1–11 to make the second shoe.

Patterns

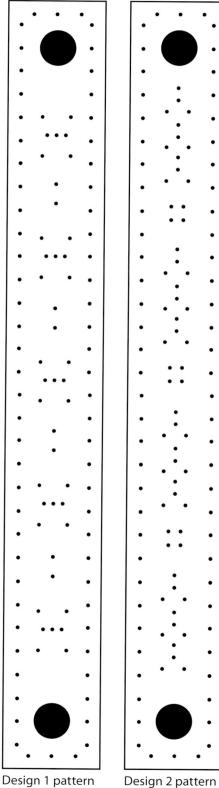

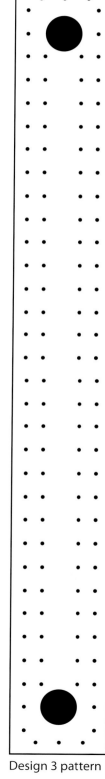

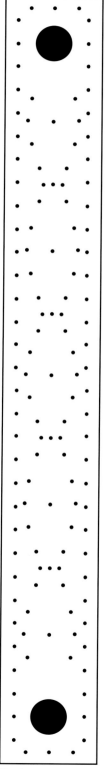

Design 1 pattern   Design 2 pattern   Design 3 pattern   Design 4 pattern

MINI SUITCASE

(page 74)

Note: The larger Mini Suitcase patterns are on pullout page P1.

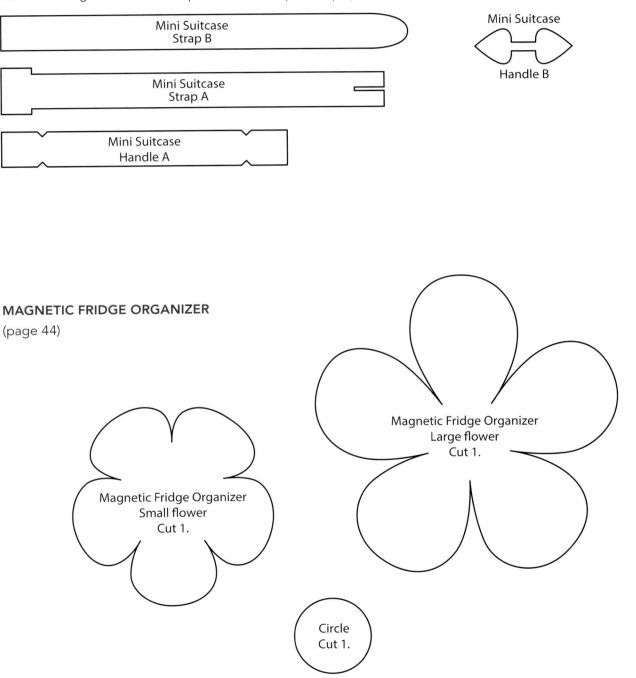

Mini Suitcase
Strap B

Mini Suitcase
Strap A

Mini Suitcase
Handle A

Mini Suitcase
Handle B

MAGNETIC FRIDGE ORGANIZER

(page 44)

Magnetic Fridge Organizer
Large flower
Cut 1.

Magnetic Fridge Organizer
Small flower
Cut 1.

Circle
Cut 1.

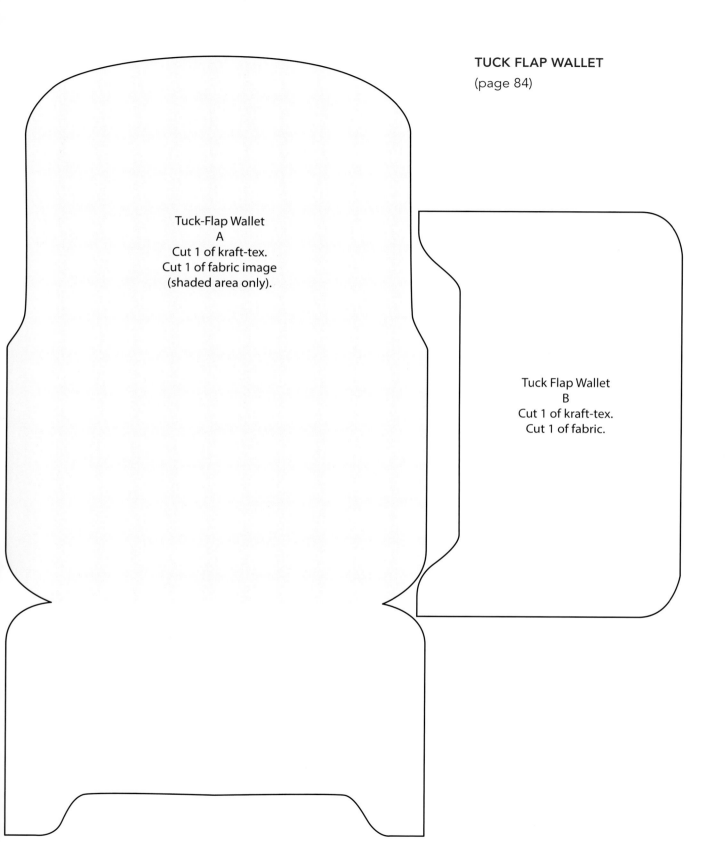

TUCK FLAP WALLET
(page 84)

Tuck-Flap Wallet
A
Cut 1 of kraft-tex.
Cut 1 of fabric image
(shaded area only).

Tuck Flap Wallet
B
Cut 1 of kraft-tex.
Cut 1 of fabric.

SNAPPY SLIM WALLET

(page 80)

Snappy Slim Wallet
A
Cut 1 of kraft-tex.

Snappy Slim Wallet
B
Cut 3 of fabric.

E (inner line)
Cut 2 from fleece interfacing.

Tuck-Flap Wallet
C
Cut 2 of kraft-tex.
Cut 1 of fabric.

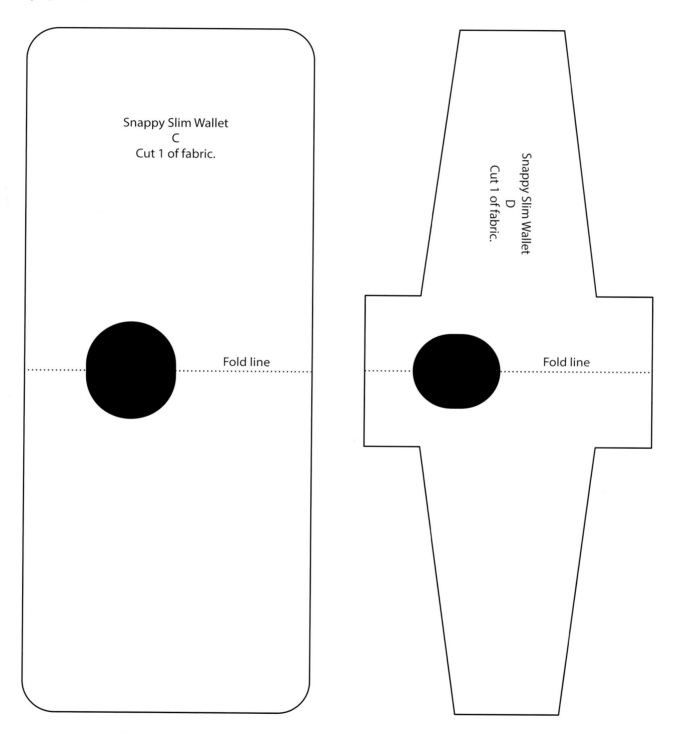

Snappy Slim Wallet
C
Cut 1 of fabric.

Fold line

Snappy Slim Wallet
D
Cut 1 of fabric.

Fold line

BABY SHOES

(page 102)

Baby Shoes
Toe
Cut 2 of main fabric.
Cut 2 of lining.

Baby Shoes
Soles
Cut 2 of outer fabric.
Cut 2 of lining.

Baby Shoes
Toe accent A
Cut 2 mirror image
of kraft-tex.

Baby Shoes
Toe accent B
Cut 2 mirror image
of kraft-tex.

Baby Shoes

Tab

Cut 2 of kraft-tex.

Baby Shoes
Heel
Cut 2 of main fabric.
Cut 2 of lining.

CELESTIAL COASTERS

(page 30)

Celestial Coasters Diamond
Cut 10 from card stock.

CUT MESH BAG

(page 88)

Note: The largest Cut Mesh Bag pattern is on pullout page P1.

Cut Mesh Bag
Handle
Cut 4 of kraft-tex.

Fold line

Cut Mesh Bag
Drawcord tab
Cut 2 of kraft-tex.

Sack fabric cutting line

Kraft-tex cutting line

Cut Mesh Bag
Base
Cut 2 of kraft-tex.
Cut 1 of fabric for sack.
(with seam allowance)